An Alternative Approach to Capital Productivity and Resource Allocation on Indian Railways

ABOUT THE AUTHOR :

b. 1945, Shri Verma did M.A in Economics with special paper in Econometrics from Ranchi University in Bihar. He was awarded the University Gold Medal for standing First in the First Division. After teaching Economics for three years in Ranchi University, he joined Indian Railway Accounts Service in 1968. He served in various capacities in the Finance department of railways at all levels viz. the Division, Zonal Headquarter and the Ministry of Railways. He worked for almost a decade in the computer centre of Indian Railways and Zambia Railways and did a consultancy assignment regarding computerisation strategy in Swaziland Railways. Shri Verma also worked in the general management branch as Additional Divisional Railway Manager in a major Division of Indian Railways. He taught Financial Management for four years in Railway Staff College, Vadodara, which is the apex training institute for officers of Indian Railways. Shri Verma has published seven papers on various aspects of railway finance. He is presently working as Group General Manager (Finance) in Rail India Technical and Economic Services Ltd.,.New Delhi, a Government of India Undertaking, which is internationally well known as leading rail transport consultants and engineers.

An Alternative Approach to

Capital Productivity and Resource Allocation on Indian Railways

K.B. VERMA
IRAS

Academic Foundation
24-A, Sriram Road, Civil Lines, Delhi - 110 054.
Phone: 232966, 233730. Fax: (011)-2911852.

First Published in 1996 by
ACADEMIC FOUNDATION
24 - A, Sriram Road, Civil Lines, Delhi - 110 054.
Tel : 232966, 233730. FAX : 91-11-2911852.

An Alternative Approach to Capital Productivity and Resource Allocation on Indian Railways
K.B. Verma
ISBN 81-7188-110-6

Laser-Typeset by
Academic Foundation's DTP Division.
Printed at Taj Press, Mayapuri, New Delhi, India.

Dedicated to
my father Shri Ram Sringar Prasad and
my mother Manorama Devi

Contents

Annexures

Foreword

RESOURCE crunch has plagued the Indian Railways always but not so severely as in the recent past. This situation is likely to continue almost perennially, making it imperative to ensure that the available scarce resources are prudently deployed. In this context any method which enables a reasonably correct measurement of the capital productivity would be most welcome. Verma's attempt at evolving an alternative approach in this area is, therefore, a laudable one.

Indian Railways do have time-tested methodology and procedures for evaluation of projects, formulation of Rolling Stock and Works Programmes and even post-commission productivity tests. If these are faithfully implemented there can be no case in which investments turn out to be infructuous or unnecessary. Unfortunately, however, the procedures and methods have come to be either ignored or implemented in the most routine and unimaginative manner leading to several cases of unwise investments. Instances are also not wanting in which data are doctored either to inflate the returns or depress the costs to get projects sanctioned to satisfy some vested interests or political compulsions! Undertaking such projects might make enormous political sense but negligible, if any, economic sense.

As ably brought out by Verma in his introductory chapter the most serious lacuna is the absence of any method or procedure to evaluate the capital productivity at the macro level. A study by RITES, on behalf of the Railway Fare & Freight Committee, had brought out the declining trend of capital output ratio of the investments on the Indian Railways in the most telling manner. The conclusion suggested was that the heavy investments made after 1985-86, either did not yield the visualised output or that investments made were on projects with a very long gestation period, which are yet to yield the projected returns. This also points to the need for having a method of appropriately evaluating on a macro basis the benefits from the substantial investments made from time to time.

Verma has argued rightly that the conventional concept of capital output ratio is either inadequate or misleading when employed to evaluate the productivity of capital on the railway system. He has attempted to develop a definition of productivity embodying both output and inhibiting factors, and developed a supplementary criteria for allocating resources amongst different zonal railways. In this approach he has introduced an indexed method in which both capital and output in a year are indexed to those in the base year: the difference between the productivity figures for the two years reflecting the difference in efficiency of capital. For record Verma has set out the capital output ratios of the zonal railways under the conventional method. After establishing that this method is not adequate for the purpose, he has developed two alternative concepts of the indexed approach *viz*. INDCOR and INDICOR — for analysing the investment data of the zonal railways. On the basis of an extensive analysis under the various methods, Verma has reached the conclusion that the indexed method is the most suitable one for evaluating the productivity of capital on the railways. He has also established that there is a discernible relationship between the investment share of a railway and its productivity. The policy implications are that since there is a definite relationship between investment share, traffic unit share, and productivity of a railway, the allocation of investible resources amongst the zonal railways should be on this basis. In other words the investment share of a zonal railway should more or less equal its traffic share. In his view this should become a part of the top down process itself and could be extended even to the Divisions after suitable date base is built up. This idea needs to be explored further.

Three noteworthy features of the study are :-

* Unlike previous studies, which concentrated on IR as a whole, this study deals with capital productivity on zonal railways.
* It has developed a conceptual framework for measuring and evaluating capital productivity more appropriate to IR situation.
* It is for the first time that some kind of criteria for guiding allocation of resources has been talked about.

As brought out by Verma in the Preface the essentials of this book are contained in his two part article titled "Marginal Productivity of Railway Investments" published in "Rail Transport", the quarterly journal of Institute of Rail Transport, India. As a matter of fact this article attracted immediate attention as is evidenced by it being referred to by the Railway Fare & Freight Committee in their Report. Verma has tried to provide a missing link in the investment appraisal and resource allocation procedures of the IR and it is hoped that it will attract the attention of the Ministry of Railways.

This monograph satisfies a felt need for a procedure to rationalise and regulate the quantum and location of investments in the most effective manner. This may not be a final answer, but it opens up an entirely new area for extensive discussion and further intensive research to fine - tune the methodology suggested. Verma will, no doubt, keep up his interest in the subject and be available for consultation, assistance and active participation in all efforts to make periodic improvements in the concepts and methodology which he has now released for public discussion and use.

A.V. Poulose

New Delhi

Former Financial Commissioner Railways and Ex-Officio Secretary to Govt. of India on this basis. In other words the investment share of a zonal railway should more or less equal its traffic share. In my view this should become a part of the top-down process itself and could be extended even to the Divisions after suitable data base is built up. This idea needs to be explored further.

Three noteworthy features of the study are:—

* Unlike previous studies, which concentrated on IR as a whole, this study deals with capital productivity on zonal railways.
* It has developed a conceptual framework for measuring and evaluating capital productivity more appropriate to IR situation.
* It is for the first time that some kind of criteria for guiding allocation of resources has been placed upon.

As brought out by Verma in the Preface the essentials of this book are contained in his two earlier articles titled "Marginal Productivity of Railway Investments" published in "Rail Transport"—the quarterly journal of Institute of Rail Transport, India. As a matter of fact this article attracted immediate attention as is evidenced by it being referred to by the Railway Fare & Freight Committee in their Report. Verma has tried to provide a missing link in the investment appraisal and resource allocation procedures of the IR and it is hoped that it will attract the attention of the Ministry of Railways.

This monograph satisfies a felt need for a procedure to rationalise and regulate the quantum and location of investments in the most effective manner. This may not be a final answer, but it opens up an entirely new vista for extensive discussion and further intensive research to fine tune the methodology suggested. Verma will, no doubt, keep up his interest in the subject and be available for consultation, assistance and active participation in all efforts to make periodic improvements in the concepts and methodology which he has now proposed for public discussion and use.

K.V. Poulose

New Delhi

Former Financial Commissioner Railways and Ex Officio Secretary to Govt. of India

Preface

IN a way this book has evolved over the last four years or so. It owes its origin to class room discussions with senior managers of Indian Railways during my very enriching four year teaching assignment with Railway Staff College, Vadodara from May, 1989 to June, 1993.

While discussing railway investments, one was not as much struck with the capital productivity scenario on the zonal railways as with conspicuous absence of a systematic study of railway investments - their nature, impact, lessons to be drawn etc. Post implementation evaluation of some important projects have been done from time to time. But there is hardly much on the capital productivity at the macro level, the total effect of the sum total of investments. A study of this aspect of investments led to the publication of two papers by me viz. 'Marginal Productivity of Railway Investments - Part 1' in 'Rail Transport' June 1991 and 'Marginal Productivity of Railway Investments - Part 2' in 'Rail Transport' September 1991, which is the journal of the Institute of Rail Transport, India. The essentials of this book are contained in the above two papers.

My colleagues in the Staff College insisted that the papers should be discussed more widely. At their instance, therefore, the main elements of the papers were discussed in various

Productivity and Financial Management Courses in 1992 and 1993, with not entirely unpredicted results. It invariably led to lively discussion. And while the concepts, the methodology and the conclusions were found acceptable, when it came to the policy implications there were quite a few unfinished 'buts'. Their hesitation was quite understandable. I learnt much from these discussions.

Further work on this problem continued, although in fits and starts and has now culminated into this book. In this book not only has the analysis been updated with latest available data, but the scope of the study itself has been widened and the conclusions retested with more stable methodology. This has only served to reconfirm the conclusions and their policy implications arrived at earlier in the two papers mentioned above.

This study is incomplete in one respect. All through, it talks in terms of volume of investments. The structure of investments, which has a strong bearing on productivity, has been referred to only in passing. In fact, structure of investments in its own right may be the subject of a separate study. Actually, not only investments but the entire gamut of railway operations is so vast and fascinating and data availability so rich that it is surprising why it has not attracted as much attention of transport economists as other modes of transport. It is hoped that this study will fill some small corner of the void. And if it generates atleast some debate amongst those concerned with rail transport, I shall consider my labour amply rewarded.

I am greatly indebted to Shri A.V.Poulose who after retirement as Financial Commissioner, Indian Railways, was Vice-Chairman 'Railway Fare and Freight Committee' 1993 and Chairman 'Railway Capital Restructuring Committee' 1994; and Smt. Mridula Krishnan, ex Economic Advisor, Ministry of Railways and Convenor of the 'Committee on Capital Output Ratio for Indian Railways' 1988 for going through the manuscript and giving their invaluable advice. The responsibility for the views expressed, however, are entirely mine.

Thanks are also due to my Personal Assistant Shri S.G. Rao who painstakingly entered the draft into the computer and then with immense patience carried out the innumerable revisions to give the book its present shape.

Needless to say this study would not have been possible without the help, understanding and encouragement from my wife Abha and my children Swati and Ankur without whose distractions, it would have, perhaps, been completed earlier.

K.B. Verma

Group General Manager (Finance),
Rail India Technical and
Economic Services Ltd.
(RITES)

P 704, Anupam Apartments,
East Arjun Nagar,
Delhi - 110 032.

1

Introduction

INDIAN Railways is one of the few railways in the world to run at profit. In 1993-94 the surplus was Rs.1806.08 crores after paying a dividend of Rs.1296.05 crores to the central exchequer and shouldering a social burden of Rs.2008.05 crores (estimated). This is certainly quite a creditable performance. But this is only one and incomplete part of the story. The above figures do not give much idea about how productively capital is being utilised by the railways.

Although talk of capital productivity is not new on Indian Railways, it is now becoming more pressing than ever before. The flow of concessional capital from Government of India (GOI) is fast dwindling. It has already fallen from 75% at one time to 14% in 1994-95. And indications are that soon it may completely dry up. Railways is, therefore, forced to raise capital from the market (IRFC Bonds) which is expensive or rely more and more on its internal resources, which is not easy. On the other hand, requirement of funds has increased to meet increasing demand for services as well as renewals and replacement of ever widening asset base. The railways is, thus, in a bind. Therefore, investments must be carefully planned and put to most productive use where returns are the quickest and the highest. But here again there is a problem. Railways is one of the most important infrastructures of the country. Besides other things, it must also serve developmental as well as social needs. Thus, returns alone cannot be the governing consideration. Trying to balance the two seemingly irreconcilable considerations has always been the fate of railway planners. It has now become more urgent.

There is inescapable need to analyse and understand railway investments in much greater detail. Unfortunately even within the railways, productivity of capital is talked about mostly in relation to individual investments or projects. Productivity of capital at the macro level i.e. what is the total impact of total investments, is not discussed. Actually, there are no statistics also to give an idea of capital productivity at the macro level. There is only one statistics which is mentioned in this context, that is the Ratio of Net Revenue to Capital-at-charge. But as shown later, as an indicator of capital productivity, this ratio is not only totally inadequate but infact misleading.

Put simply, productivity of capital means the output generated per unit of capital employed i.e. output capital ratio or its inverse capital output ratio. Usually, the numerator and denominator of this ratio are in terms of money value. This enables a comparison of the capital productivity of two firms, industries or sectors as diverse as power and transport. But taking railways' output in terms of money i.e. its earnings would be erroneous. Actually, railways, particularly in India, has some special features which sets it apart from other industries. And these features have a direct bearing on its capital productivity.

a) First the use of money value to represent output. In most industries the price that a commodity is able to command is its value and the income derived by its sale is the value of output of the company. Not so in railways. In many sectors like bulk goods, long distance passengers etc. the demand for railways' services is so inelastic that it gives railways a near monopolistic position. It could thus charge considerably more price for its services. But it does not do so. Not only that, in many cases railways is compelled to charge even less than the cost. There is also an element of heavy cross-subsidisation, some services are charged more to meet, atleast partly, the losses on some other services.

Thus, railways earnings cannot be taken as a measure of its output and hence should not be relied upon for computation of capital output ratio.

b) A more dependable indicator of output can be the physical output. But once money is given up as a measure of output, innumerable problems are encountered. Not only capital productivity of two industries e.g. textile and steel, cannot be compared, even within the same industry e.g. textiles, multi-product firms become incomparable. In such a situation, the only solution, though not an entirely satisfactory one, is to adopt a system of weightages to convert different kinds of outputs into one common denominator. In the railways also a similar method has been adopted. But more about this later.

c) In case of most industries the consumer can move to 'B' if his demand is not satisfied at 'A'. It is also possible to meet the demand at place 'X' from place 'Y' or 'Z'. In other words, there is to a large extent mobility or transferability of both demand and supply. In the case of railways, this is not so. The demand must be satisfied where it originates. To clarify further if there is demand for wagons at place 'A', the service must be provided at place 'A', otherwise the traffic will most likely be lost.

d) In case of losses other firms can cut down production or, atleast theoretically, even close down. No such option is available to the Indian railways. On the contrary, even upgrading or expanding such services becomes unavoidable. In such cases, capital productivity is bound to be low. Still investments will have to be made.

Even with the above constraints capital productivity must be of paramount consideration. Investments must be made based on productivity consideration alone. One way of reconciling this may, perhaps, be to define productivity itself in such a manner that it embodies both output and such other conditions which inhibit output. Once this is done, productivity may legitimately be taken to govern investments.

The present study attempts to develop such a definition of productivity and then proceeds to develop a criteria which may be adopted for allocation of resources amongst different zonal railways and thereby determine investments.

2

Indian Railways

BEFORE coming to the main subject, it is necessary to talk about certain features of Indian Railways (IR) in order to enable those not familiar with IR to appreciate the discussion.

By any stretch of imagination IR is a vast organisation. With a route length of 62,486 KM it is the largest railway system in the world, after the break up of erstwhile Soviet Union. With a work force 1.65 million employees it is the second biggest industrial employer in the world, next only to the Chinese railways. But apart from size alone, IR often boasts of being one of the few railways in the world to run at profit enabling it to pay annual dividend to the Government of India (GOI). The only subsidy it receives from GOI is in the form of concessional capital which meets only part of its investment requirements. This also has been declining over the years as a percentage of total annual investments of IR. On the other hand the estimated loss on account of running uneconomic services which are called Social Burdens has been increasing every year.

On the whole, therefore, IR can be said to be one of the few enterprises of the Government of India which is profitable. It not only bears heavy social burdens but also pays a return on the capital invested.

Administratively IR is a three tier structure with the Railway Board, which is also the Ministry of Railways in the Government of India (GOI), at the apex. The Railway Board has substantial administrative and financial powers not generally available to other Government Departments or Public Sector Undertakings (PSUs). It is the only department of the GOI whose Budget is presented to the Parliament separately from that of the GOI although figures of railway earnings and expenditure are incorporated in GOI budget also.

The entire Indian Railway (IR) system is divided into zones - nine at present - which are separate geographical units. A list of the nine railway zones at present is in Annexure-1. Administratively and financially each zone is a complete unit and it has its own Earnings Budget and Expenditure Budget. Each zone is further divided into geographical Divisions. A Division is an exact replica of the set up at the zonal level except that while it has its own Expenditure Budget, its Earnings Budget is not on the same pattern as that of the zone. However, the details of this are outside the scope of our present study.

The Expenditure Budget of IR is presented to the Parliament under 16 Heads of Demand, as at Annexure-2. Each Head of Demand deals with either a specific function or a group of identifiable functions of the organisation. Here, we are concerned with only one Head of Demand which deals with investments i.e. Demand 16 - Assets Acquisition, Construction and Replacement.

In Indian Railways capital expenditure or investments can be financed either through external resources i.e. loan from GOI or through internal resources generated by the railways. The internal resources are in the form of Funds viz. Depreciation Reserve Fund (DRF), Development Fund (DF), Accident Compensation Safety and Passenger Amenities Fund (ACSPF), and Open Line Works Revenue or OLW(R) which is not a Fund. A Fund is one into which some monies are put and from which some monies are withdrawn thereby leaving a balance which earns interest. OLW(R) is not a Fund. The actual expenditure which falls in the category of OLW(R) is met from internal revenues of railways. With effect from 1.4.1993 ACSPF has been discontinued and a new fund called Capital Fund has been created. Loan from GOI is a non-refundable loan given at a concessional rate of interest called Dividend, currently 7% per annum. The rate of Dividend is decided by Parliament through Railway Convention Committee every five years. This five year period coincides with the Five Year Plans. Only investments financed out of such loan are called capital and add to the cumulative capital-at-charge of railways. Investments financed out of internal resources of the railways, though of capital nature, do not add to the capital-at-charge. It is important to remember that what is called capital or capital-at-charge is not the entire investment of railways.

The amount of capital or budgetary support which can be provided by GOI is decided every year by the Ministry of Finance. And the amount of money which can be put into each of the Funds is approved by the Parliament based on the recommendations of the Convention Committee. Not all kinds of investments can be met from all the Funds. Each Fund has a specific purpose. And the type of expenses which can be met out of capital or from these Funds or from OLW(R) is subject to the approval of the Parliament on the recommendations of the Convention Committee. The rules regarding which type of expenditure can be met from which fund have been codified in IR Finance Code Volume-1.

Expenses of capital nature have been also classified into what are known as Plan Heads e.g. New Lines (Construction), Gauge Conversion, Rolling Stock, Staff Quarters etc. A complete list of the Plan Heads and the sources of funds from which they can be financed is given at Annexure-3. Needless to say the Plan Heads give a reasonably good idea of the structure of investments.

The annual investment plan of the railways is compiled in a document called Works, Machinery and Rolling Stock Programme or in short the Works Programme, also called the Pink Book because of the colour of the cover. It is a part of the Budget Papers submitted to Parliament. It lists all items of investment individually whether on-going or proposed to be taken up as a new item in the year under consideration. The items continue to be shown in this document till completion. For each item of investment the total estimated cost, the amount spent upto date, amount proposed for investment in the current year, the balance carried forward and the source of funding are given. Such investments whose estimated cost are above a particular limit, presently Rs.50.00 lakhs, are listed individually. For the others only a 'Lump sum' provision is shown. Details of these are required to be maintained by the Zonal Railways themselves. Even in the zonal railway head offices, itemwise details of works costing above Rs.10.00 lakhs only are required to be maintained and those below this amount are shown under a 'Lump Sum' provision the details of which are in turn required to be maintained by the concerned Divisions.

The exercise to prepare the Works Programme starts one year before the Budget time i.e. for the Budget to be presented in February/March 1996, the exercise to prepare the Works Programme would start in May 1995. Detailed justification for each New Item is prepared and financially evaluated. Detailed guidelines for justification of various kinds of investments, preparation of estimates, financial evaluation etc. exist. Fund requirement for the current year whether for new works or on-going works is to be realistically estimated. This leads to the document called Preliminary Works Programme (PWP) and is submitted by the zonal railways to the Railway Board. The PWP of each railway is discussed by the Railway Board with a high power team of each railway individually. And then the Works Programme of each railway is finalised which is called the Final Works Programme (FWP). This document then forms part of the Budget documents of that railway as its Works, Machinery and Rolling Stock Programme.

The above interaction between the zonal railway and the Railway Board is replicated between the Divisions and the Headquarters office of the zonal railways.

Before the work of preparing PWP of a railway reaches an advanced stage, the Railway Board after consultations with the Planning Commission and the Ministry of Finance gives a Fund Indication to the zonal railways - that is the amounts that can be expected under various sources of financing so that the railways can frame their proposals accordingly. Consultations with the Planning Commission and Ministry of Finance ensures that railways' investment plans are in tune with overall investment strategy of the Government of India and requirements of the economy. It also gives an idea to the railways regarding the Budgetary support i.e. loan from GOI that may be expected. Other issues also require the approval of Ministry of Finance e.g. the amount of loan that railways may be allowed to raise from the market through the Indian Railway Finance Corporation (IRFC), the interest that will have to be paid to the public on the IRFC Bond, whether the interest will be tax-free etc.

It may thus be seen that railways' planning process is a truly top-to-bottom and bottom-to-top approach. Its investment plans emerge after rigorous analysis starting from the Divisions going right up to the Ministry of Railways and in consultation with the Ministry of Finance and the Planning Commission. Railways investment plans are, however, not subject to scrutiny by the Public Investment Board though of late, proposals/ projects costing Rs.50.00 crores or more are required to be cleared by an expanded Board including Secretary Expenditure and Secretary Planning from the Ministry of Finance and later on approved by the Cabinet Committee on Economic Affairs. On the whole, Railways enjoy more independence than other Government departments or Public Sector Undertakings.

A word about the structure of accounts is also necessary. The structure given below has been framed in a manner as to clearly bring out the composition of important terms used in this study.

1. EARNINGS	Amount (Rs.)
a) Traffic Earnings	
Goods	500.00
Coaching	200.00
Sundries	100.00
Gross Earnings	800.00
(-) Traffic Suspense	40.00
Gross Traffic Receipts	760.00
b) Miscellaneous Receipts	
Receipts from Subsidised companies	50.00
Railway Recruitment Boards	10.00
Other Miscellaneous Receipts	10.00
Surcharge on Passengers	5.00
Total Miscellaneous Receipts	75.00

2. EXPENDITURE	
a) Working Expenses	
Ordinary Working Expenses (Demands 3 to 13)	500.00
Appropriation to Depreciation Reserve Fund	200.00
Appropriation to Pension Fund	50.00
Total Working Expenditure	750.00
b) Miscellaneous Expenditure	
Subsidy to Worked Lines	5.00
Demands 1 & 2	10.00
Appropriation to Pension Fund (for Demand 1 & 2)	5.00
Appropriation to ACSPF	5.00
Total Miscellaneous Expenditure	25.00

c)	Payment to General Revenue		
	Dividend on Total Capital		40.00
	Grant in lieu of Passenger Fare Tax		10.00
	Contribution to Safety Works Fund		10.00
	Total Payment to General Revenue		60.00
(-)	Compensation for Working Losses on Strategic Lines	12.00	
(-)	Concession in Dividend Payments	3.00	15.00
	Net Payment to General Revenue		45.00

Then,

Net Revenue

= (Gross Tfc. Receipt + Total Misc.Receipts) – (Total Working Exp. + Total Misc. Exp.)

= (Rs.760.00 + Rs.75.00) – (Rs.750.00 + Rs.25.00)

= Rs.60.00

$$\text{Operating Ratio} = \frac{\text{Total Working Expenses}}{\text{Gross Earnings}} \times 100$$

$$= \frac{\text{Rs.}750.00}{\text{Rs.}800.00} \times 100$$

= 93.75%

Surplus/Deficit = Net Revenue – Net Payment to General Revenue

= Rs.60.00 – Rs.45.00

= Rs.15.00

The figures above are purely imaginary, adopted just to explain the structure.

It may be seen from Annexure-2 that expenditure on Demand 1 'Railway Board' and Demand 2 'Research, Audit and Miscellaneous Establishment' is common expenditure on behalf of all railways and is not much dependent upon the quantum of work on the zonal railways, hence it is kept separate from 'Working Expenses'.

The above terms as well as their components will be relevant for subsequent analysis.

Two other terms have been used in this study - Loan Account and Block Account. Loan Account records all investments financed out of loan from GOI i.e. capital-at-charge. Block Account records investments from all sources including loan. The following sentence from Appendix-VII of Explanatory Memorandum on the Railway Budget clarifies.

> "On the other hand, the Block Account - forming an annexure to the annual Appropriation Accounts for Indian Railways indicates the total including the value of assets financed from the Development Fund, Accident Compensation Safety and Passenger Amenities Fund and Revenue as also the "improvement element", of the cost of assets financed from Depreciation Reserve Fund."

The Block Account may thus be said to represent the value of all investments on Indian Railways. With this background we may now proceed to the main subject under discussion.

3

Capital Productivity

Ratio of Net Revenue to Capital-at-charge

ON Indian Railways the productivity of investment at the macro level is usually measured by a ratio called the ratio of Net Revenue to Capital-at-charge, which is taken to be akin to rate of return. This ratio is calculated for individual zonal railways as well as Indian Railways as a whole. But, this ratio has severe limitations and does not really reflect the productivity of capital.

i) As would be seen from the structure of Accounts explained in Chapter-2, Net Revenue can be artificially manipulated by just deciding to put less money into the Depreciation Reserve Fund and the Pension Fund in any given year which would reduce Total Working Expenses and thus increase Net Revenue. This is possible because appropriation to the Funds are neither based on any set formulae nor have any bearing on the expenditure from these funds in any year.

ii) Because of its monopolistic position Indian Railways can, in any year, increase fares and freights and thereby show better Net Revenue, without in any way having actually improved its capital productivity.

iii) Capital-at-charge is the investment from loan capital

only. This is not the entire investment. And since Gross Earnings, on which Net Revenue is based, derives benefit from investments from all sources and not only from loan capital, it is the entire investment which should be considered if productivity of investments is to be realistically evaluated.

Thus the ratio of Net Revenue to Capital-at-charge does not in any way show the productivity of investments. This point is now becoming more important because of falling Government of India loan to railways, increasing investment from internal resources and use of assets acquired on lease from Indian Railway Finance Corporation which do not form part of railway's investments at all.

Capital Output Ratio

Therefore, some other ratio needs to be adopted. Capital output ratio is one such ratio. However, certain clarification regarding capital and output need to be given before the capital output ratio is adopted as a measure of capital productivity.

Output is only one of the purposes of investment. Other purposes may be - renewals and replacements, improving efficiency, reducing working costs, development of less developed areas, meeting statutory requirements, research, welfare and so on. Which of these is important, would depend upon the objectives of the organisation itself. But, since Indian Railways is not a public utility service like medical services, education etc., all or almost all investments must directly or indirectly sooner or later - and more directly than indirectly and sooner than later - must lead to increase in output. It has been shown later that even renewals and replacement expenditure must be governed by the requirements of output only. The aim of railway planning and investment policies, therefore, must be increase in output.

Further, capital is not the only factor of production. Classical economists recognise land, labour, capital and organisation as the main factors of production. Of late, information and technology have been added to the list, although the classical economists would have preferred to club them with organisation and capital respectively. But all said and done labour is an equally important factor of production.

This study, however, talks about productivity of capital only. This is because of two reasons. First, it is possible to argue that improvement in productivity of labour comes about mainly because of better tools and plant, equipment, machinery, automation, training etc., in other words more induction of capital rather than something ascribable to labour itself.

In fact it is also believed in certain quarters that increased productivity of staff on railways - as reflected by output per employee - is more because of better rolling stock, signals and track etc. i.e. induction of more capital rather than anything else.

Secondly, particularly in the context of a developing and labour surplus economy like India, capital is much more scarce than labour. Hence, although the entire output cannot be really ascribed to capital alone it is quite in order to do so and talk in terms of productivity of capital rather than other factors of production. Considering other factors would only cloud the issues.

Committee on Capital Output Ratio

Not much study on capital output ratio of Indian Railways has been done. Some work on the capital output ratios of different sectors of the Indian economy has been done and in that context capital output ratio of Indian Railways also calculated e.g. "Behaviour of Capital Output Ratio in Indian Economy" by Indian Institute of Management, Ahmedabad, the study of Capital Output Ratios of Indian economy conducted by a Working Group of Planning Coimmission in 1985 etc. But that is about all. The only exclusive work on capital output ratio of Indian Railways has been by a Committee set up by the Ministry of Railways as a sequel to the recommendations of the Railway Reforms Committee, 1984. The Report of the 'Committee on Capital Output Ratio for Indian Railways' was submitted in July, 1988.

This Committee recommended the Average Capital Output

Ratio concept as the one relevant for Indian Railways, developed a methodology for calculation of Average Capital Output Ratio (ACOR) and Incremental Capital Output Ratio (ICOR) for Indian Railways and computed these ratios for various years between 1965-66 and 1985-86.

But all this was for Indian Railways as a whole.

Then the Committee made the following observations —

Para 3.19

"The COR/ICOR trends for the railways, if analysed properly at micro and macro levels would go a long way in providing Railway Management suitable guidance for *inter zonal and inter-departmental resource allocation* and at the same time would also help in the perspective planning and economic modelling" (emphasis mine).

Para 6.7

"..... The specific areas of new investment call for thorough examination taking into consideration all the relevant alternatives for achieving the desired results and this is possible only if we investigate the productivity trends and analyse the capial output ratio at micro level i.e. *at zonal and departmental levels.*" (emphasis mine).

It would not be entirely erroneous to conclude from the above, therefore, that —

(i) the Committee was not fully satisfied with the existing methodology of resource allocation, and

(ii) the Committee felt that an analysis of the Capital Output Ratios of different zones (such as Northern Railway, Southern Railway etc.) and different departments (such as Civil Engineering, Mechanical Engineering etc.) would go a long way in providing suitable guidelines for resource allocation.

This opinion of the Committee is important.

One clarification is necessary. By suggesting that capital

output ratios of different departments should be analysed, perhaps what the Committee actually had in mind was that capital output ratios of different functions or rather different groups of assets should be analysed. For example the Mechanical Engineering department deals with Locomotives, Coaches, Wagons, Workshops etc. It would, therefore, be more appropriate to analyse the capital productivity of these groups of assets separately rather than Mechanical Engineering department as a whole.

However, the Committee did not proceed to analyse or calculate the capital output ratios of different zones or departments/functions. They dealt only with the capital output ratio of Indian Railway as a whole.

In the present study calculation and analysis of capital output ratios of different zones has been attempted. In this respect the present study may be said to be the logical extension of the work of the Committee on Capital Output Ratios. But the similarity ends here. In fact, there is a fundamental difference between this study and the study of the Committee. In this study an entirely different concept of capital productivity has been followed and a different methodology for its evaluation has been adopted.

Here, it is necessary to identify the main features of the methodology adopted by the Committee. These are

a) Assets of different kinds were divided into certain categories.

b) They were then revalued to a particular base year.

c) For the purpose of revaluation different price indices were used.

d) Output was measured in terms of Equated Net Tonne Kilometers (NTKM). The weights adopted for 'Equating' were the same as that recommended by Productivity Linked Bonus Committee (1985), i.e. 1:1, 1:0.5 and 1:0.25 for Goods, Passenger (non-suburban) and Passenger (suburban) traffic.

e) Output in terms of 'value added' was also computed.

f) ACOR and ICOR were then calculated for both types of output.

The above methodology has not been found suitable because of the following reasons.

a) It has a number of subjective elements and is open to debate particularly on the adoption of inflator/deflator indices for revaluation of capital to a particular year, the computation of 'value added' and so on.

b) By converting different types of output (e.g. Passenger KMs, Freight KMs etc.) to a common denominator, i.e. Traffic Unit, through a system of weightages the Committee has been able to overcome one problem - i.e. of multi product. But this is not enough. This question has been discussed later in greater detail while discussing the effect of institutional factors. Suffice to say here that this conversion alone does not take care of many other factors which have a bearing on the capital output ratio. One such factor is difference in characteristics of different products in the same product group e.g. within the same product group freight kilometers NTKMs of originating/terminating traffic and cross traffic are not the same as the former requires more investment than the latter. One way to resolve this problem is to develop some more weightages. But besides the fact that developing weightages is a complex and often unsatisfactory affair, it may turn out to be an endless exercise to cater to various kinds of differences. The alternative method of measuring capital productivity as suggested in this study eliminates the need for such weightages. Only the first level weightage has been used i.e. for converting different kinds of output into one common denominator Traffic Units.

c) Revaluation of assets to a base year is really not necessary for the limited purpose of evaluating the Capital Output ratio of zonal railways for resource allocation purposes. Valuation of capital of different years to a base year is necessary only for a temporal comparison i.e. if capital output ratios of different years are required to be compared to find whether the productivity of capital has improved or deteriorated. But for resource allocation purposes comparison of capital output ratios after revaluation of capital is not necessary. In fact since the time period involved is the same for all the railways the same inflator/deflator indices will be used, hence revaluation of capital would produce the same results. The results may be different only if the structure of capital of different railways undergoes a change. But then this is precisely one of the factors which is the subject of the study i.e. whether the amount and structure of capital is more intensive than actually warranted. In this study therefore revaluation of capital to a base year has not been done.

Present Study

In nutshell, this study proceeds in the following manner.

First, the conceptual framework is established in Chapter-4. It has been shown why the conventional definition of capital output ratio is not applicable to IR. An alternative concept has then been suggested. It has then been said that whether the capital output ratio is calculated on the conventional concept or the proposed concept, after calculating it the next problem would be to evaluate it. Further, if the purpose of the comparison is only to find out whether ratio of railway A is better than that of railway B then a straight comparison would be quite adequate. But then it also needs to be found out whether the ratio represents a satisfactory situation or otherwise. For this a comparison with some kind of yardstick is necessary. In this chapter, a yardstick has also been developed and a slightly different method of comparison adopted.

In Chapter-5 the capital output ratios of the zonal railways over a period of time have been compared. It is found that the inter-railway differences are not explainable by traditionally accepted reasons and it has been suggested that perhaps the reason could be the way investment decisions are taken. One of them being rather disproportionate concern with micro considerations to the extent of neglect of the macro considerations.

In order to develop a criteria, which can be used to guide the macro consideration, an attempt has been made to see whether any relationship exists between the output of a railway as a share of total output of Indian Railways and its investments as a share of total investments of Indian Railways and its resultant productivity. Such a relationship has in fact been found.

Analysis regarding the above relationship in respect of investments from capital-at-charge only has been done in Chapter-6. This analysis has been separately done for the two conventional concepts of capital output ratio as well as the two proposed concepts. And then the results have been combined to see whether the relationships observed still hold good.

As already mentioned, capital is not the only source of investment. Investments are made from other sources of finance also. Output is the result of investment from all sources of fund. Therefore a capital output ratio which does not take into account investments from all sources, would present a distorted picture of productivity. In Chapter-7, therefore, all types of investments taken in entirety have been considered. In addition, the nature and effect of renewals and replacement expenditure, which forms a very large part of investments and is increasing every year, is discussed in a little more detail.

The results obtained in Chapter-6 for 'Capital-at-charge' and Chapter-7 for 'Total Investments' have been combined in Chapter-8 and the main conclusions of the study have been drawn.

The policy implications of the conclusions on allocation of investible resources amongst the zonal railways have been discussed in Chapter-9.

It needs to be clarified that the Production Units of the railways have been kept outside the scope of this study.

Thus in this study -

* The capital / output ratios of the zonal railways has been calculated based on the conventional concept of capital/output ratio.

* It has been shown that in the context of Indian Railways the conventional concept of capital/output ratio is not applicable.

* Two alternative concepts of capital/output ratio based on indexed approach have been developed. It has been suggested that this approach is more relevant.

* An alternative standard for evaluating capital/output ratio has been developed and the capital productivities of the zonal railway evaluated according to this standard.

* Although the Indexed approach has been recommended the relationship between investments and productivity of capital on the zonal railways has been examined on the basis of all four concepts of Capital Output Ratio.

* A particular relationship between investment share of a railway and its productivity has been found.

* Based on the observed relationship a criterion for the allocation of resources amongst different railways has been suggested.

Methodology

Some explanation regarding methodology followed in this study will help to put matters into proper perspective.

The aim of the study is to find whether a macro criteria can be developed for determining allocation of investible funds amongst the different zonal railways.

For this purpose, first a hypothesis is made that - the best results on capital productivity are obtained when investment share of a railway is more or less equal to its share of output i.e. traffic units. This hypothesis is evaluated (Chapter-6, 7 and 8) and found to be valid. It is then suggested (Chapter-9) that this relationship may be adopted as an enveloping macro criteria for resource allocation amongst the zonal railways.

The hypothesis is evaluated in the following manner.

It will be seen from the above that there are three main elements in the analysis, viz.

* Traffic Unit share i.e. the ratio of traffic units of a railway to the total traffic units of Indian railways,
* Investment share i.e. the ratio of investments on a railway to the total investment on Indian railways, and
* Capital productivity. Capital productivity is being calculated separately for investments from capital, also called Capital-at-charge, and Total Investment from all sources of funds. Further, Productivity is being calculated according to two conventional concepts viz. Average Capital Output Ratio (ACOR) and Incremental Capital Output Ratio (ICOR) and two proposed alternative methods viz. Indexed Capital Output Ratio (INDCOR) and Indexed Incremental Capital Output Ratio (INDICOR).

The type of relationship - HIGH, EQUAL or LOW between the first two elements has an effect on the last one. The relationship has been examined in different time periods, say for example 1970-71 to 1980-81. Then,

— The first element is taken from data for the base year, in this case 1970-71.

— As regards the second element, two figures are required - investments upto the base year and investments during the period under consideration. Data for the latter, however, are taken depending upon the type of productivity being calculated. If ACOR or INDCOR is being calculated then the investments up to the current year, in this case 1980-81, is taken. If ICOR or INDICOR is being calculated only the incremental investments between the base year and the current year are taken.

— For the third element i.e. capital productivity the

investment and traffic unit figures are taken in the same manner as for the second element.

It will be seen that traffic unit share and the other two elements have been taken at two different time periods. This is logical. Since the aim of the study is to find a macro criteria for resource allocation in future, it is necessary to relate productivity in a future time period to factors in a prior period of time. Only then, decision for future can be based on behaviour of factors in the present time period. Secondly, taking two time periods gives cognisance to the fact that there is a time lag between investments and output. It is not possible to say what is the length of this time lag at the macro level. But as would be seen later many different time lengths have been taken for study and the hypothesis evaluated.

In this study data for the period 1970-71 to 1992-93 has been taken which not only gives a reasonably broad time spectrum but also an investment spectrum varying from placid investments to quite heavy investments. This time frame has been divided into two periods viz. 1970-71 to 1988-89 as Period-1 and 1988-89 to 1992-93 as Period-2, 1988-89 being the dividing line between the two. There is no particular significane in this. It is only that when the study was first done in 1991 data upto 1988-89 only was available. Study for Period-2 has been done now when data upto 1992-93 is available. But, this has had some unintended benefits. First, it has been possible to have different lengths of time slices. Secondly, and more important, in Period-2 a slightly different methodology has been followed in taking the traffic unit and investment figures for the base year. This has been explained further in Chapter-6.

Period-1 has been further sub-divided into different time slices viz. - 1970-71 to 1980-81 i.e. 10 years, 1980-81 to 1988-89 i.e. 8 years and the whole period 1970-71 to 1988-89 i.e. 18 years. In Period-2 there is only one 5 year time slice from 1988-89 to 1992-93. Analysis in each time slice has been done separately for Capital-at-charge and Total Investment and for the four methods of calculating capital productivity as explained above.

In Period-1, under each method of capital productivity the results of different slices have been added to get

* Railway-wise Productivity Matrix, and
* Productivity Matrix, irrespective of railways,

Then, the two matrices of all the methods have been added to get irrespective of method,

* Railway-wise Productivity Matrix, and
* Productivity Matrix, irrespective of railways.

This has been separately done for Capital-at-charge and Total Investments.

The same scheme has been followed in Period-2.

However, in case of Total Investment Period 1 is limited to 1980-81 to 88-89 only for want of ready availability of necessary data for the prior period.

Finally, the results of the two periods have been combined in Chapter-8.

It will be seen from the above structure that many different scenario have been adopted for study - different kinds of investment, different methods, different time slices varying in length from 5 years to 18 years. Each scenario has its own special characteristic. But conclusions leading to policy implications should not be based on phenomenon dependent on vicissitudes of circumstances. As far as possible the extraordinary factors should be eliminated. This is sought to be done by adding the results of different scenario to obtain Productivity Matrices such that peculiarities of each scenario, at least theoretically, get evened out. Then the conclusions drawn can be said to be more reliable.

It needs to be mentioned that what is central to the study is the evaluation of the hypothesis and not any particular method or time slice itself. And if different methods, different time slices and/or their mix show similar trends then the validity of the trend gets further strengthened, the hypothesis gets further reinforced. As has happened in this case.

4

Measuring Capital Productivity

IN this Chapter the conceptual framework is explained.

Conventional concept

Capital/output ratio has been defined by economists in various ways depending upon the definitions of capital and output. But all of them fall in one of the two categories viz. the Averge Capital Output Ratio or the Incremental Capital Output Ratio. These two concepts can be better explained in the following manner.

Let

BT = Traffic Units (TU) in Base Year

BC = Capital in Base Year

IT = Incremental TU between Base Year and Current Year.

IC = Incremental Capital between Base Year and Current Year.

In this study —

i) Capital means all investments of capital nature, unless otherwise specified.

ii) Although the word used is capital/output ratio, what is

implied is output /capital ratio.

iii) Output is measured in physical units, not financial terms. For the definition of Traffic Units (TU) please see 'Annexure 1- Glossary of Terms'.

Then, the conventional concepts of capital output ratio can be defined as —

a) Average Capital Output Ratio (ACOR), also called just Capital Output Ratio (COR).

$$\text{ACOR in base year} = \frac{BT}{BC}$$

$$\text{ACOR in Current year} = \frac{BT + IT}{BC + IC}$$

b) Incremental Capital Output Ratio (ICOR)

$$\text{ICOR in Current year} = \frac{IT}{IC}$$

Let us now apply these concepts to the nine zones of Indian Railways.

For the period 1970-71/88-89 and 1988-89/92-93 the ACOR and ICOR of different zonal rialways arranged in descending order are shown in Table 1. Base data are in Annexures-20 and 21. It needs to be mentioned that here the figures for capital-at-charge only have been taken, for want of ready availability of data regarding investments from DRF, DF,ACSPF and OLWR for the period 1970-71 to 1980-81 :

The following points in Table below may be noted

* Inter railway differences
* Difference between the highest and the lowest
* Deviation from the IR average
* Change of ranking of different railways in different years

Table 1

	ACOR						ICOR		
	70-71		*88-89*		*92-93*		*70-71/88-89*		*88-89/92-93*
WR	10.15	WR	4.16	WR	3.44	CR	3.11	NR	1.70
NE	7.85	CR	3.80	CR	3.08	WR	3.07	CR	1.41
SC	7.12	NR	3.73	NR	2.62	NR	2.89	SE	0.91
CR	6.05	NE	3.28	ER	2.52	ER	2.19	ER	0.83
NR	5.87	ER	3.04	NE	2.36	SE	2.12	WR	0.62
ER	4.52	SE	2.79	SE	2.29	NE	1.96	SC	0.58
SR	3.99	SC	2.77	SC	2.06	SC	1.91	NE	0.56
SE	3.95	SR	2.07	SR	1.41	SR	1.24	NF	0.22
NF	2.46	NF	1.39	NF	.98	NF	0.87	SR	0.20
IR	5.54	IR	3.13	IR	2.39	IR	2.31	IR	0.74

It must be cautioned that the comparison of a railway in two time periods e.g. ACOR of CR in 1970-71 and 1992-93, would not be valid as the capital costs have not been converted to a base year. However, ranking of railways in two time periods would show the relative position of capital productivity on different railways in those two years. Thus while it would not be correct to compare the Average Capital Output ratio of CR in 1970-71 and 1992-93 and say that it deteriorated from 6.05 to 3.08, it would be quite correct to say that in 1970-71 CR ranked fourth and in 1992-93 ranked second in productivity of capital.

Having made the above comparison based on the conventional concepts of productivity, it is now of importance to see whether the above two concepts can be reasonably applied to the zonal railways for the purpose of finding out the productivity of capital on different railways.

Applicability on Indian Railways

Economic theory demands that the Marginal Productivity of capital on all railways should be equal in order to achieve the best deployment of capital. This implies that if Rs.100.00 invested in SE gives an output of 50 TUs then Rs.100.00 invested in NE should also give an output of 50 TUs to achieve the best deployment of capital.

Is it justified to expect this in the context of the zonal railways? The answer would depend upon whether output means the same thing on two zonal railways.

It is generally believed that Rs.100.00 invested in a freight oriented railway would give higher TUs than that invested in a passenger oriented railway. But this ipso facto cannot lead to the conclusion that use of capital on the passenger oriented railway is less efficient than that on the freight oriented railway.

Here a distinction needs to be made between productivity of capital and efficinecy of capital. Productivity of capital just means output per unit of capital. Efficiency of capital would also involve considering whether in the given circumstances it is possible to produce more output. Thus, besides the physical assets, the circumstances within which the physical assets are operating would become equally important. In the example above, capital used on the passenger oriented railway may be less productive in the sense that it produces less TUs, but it need not necessarily follow that it is being less efficiently used. It is quite possible that in spite of very judicious investment decisions and efficient utilisation of assets the resultant output in a passenger oriented railway may inherently be less than that on a freight oriented railway. Therefore, productivity considerations would require that investments be made only in the freight oriented railway at least until its marginal productivity, obeying the law of Diminishing Returns, becomes equal to that in the passenger oriented railway. But this is not practicable. Investments must be made in the passenger oriented railway also to meet the growing demand. At the same time it is also necessary to guard against avoidable overcapitalisation. For example a passenger oriented railway, taking the above plea of being inherently less output generating may tend to justify even expensive non-productive investments.

This leads to a conflict between pure productivity consideration, ground realities and the need to prevent overcapitalisation. None of these can be ignored. It may be seen that the conflict arises primarily if an unit of output on a freight oriented railway is taken to be the same as an unit of output on a passenger oriented railway though in actual fact they are quite different. The capital and working cost requirements of the two are not the same.

One way of resolving this conflict may be to define the two kinds of output viz. Freight Net Tonne KM (NTKM) and Passenger KMs (PKM) in such a way that they become comparable. Two such attempts have been made in the past. Earlier non-suburban PKMs were converted into NTKM by adopting a weightage of factor 0.71, this being the difference between Specific Fuel Consumption of freight and non-suburban passenger traffic. Suburban passenger traffic was ignored. This method was found unsatisfactory. Therefore, the Productivity Linked Bonus Reveiw Committee (Sept.1985) suggested 1:1 1:0.5 and 1:0.25 for converting NTKM, Non-suburban PKM and Suburban PKM into an Equated NTKM (or Traffic Units) which has been adopted in this study also. This was based on differences in working cost and earnings potential of the three kinds of traffic.

But this is still not adequate. What the above formulae does is to take into account the difference between NTKM and PKM. But again NTKM on a largely carrying railway like CR or NR is different from NTKM on an originating railway like ER or SE railway. The capital and working cost requirements of the two are different. A way must, therefore, be found to further correct the Equated NTKM (or TU) to take this into account. Not only this. Actually, some way must be found of incorporating all factors of inter-railway differences over which a railway has no control but which affect capital output ratio, for example difference in gauge mix. One way of doing this would be to build a comprehensive system of weightages. But any system of weightages designed to take care of all such factors may prove to be not only unsatisfactory but also an endless exercise.

It is possible to steer clear of most of these problems by defining capital productivity in a way which brings out how carefully a railway is acquiring its assets, structuring them, replacing them, utilising them etc. in relation to its own individual peculiarities, which in fact is the primary purpose of any productivity evaluation.

The Indexed Approach

The above argument, for the sake of simplicity, has been built around inter-railway differences in traffic-mix. But this is not the only element of inherent inter-railway differences leading to differences in productivity. Actually output may be said to be the result of two sets of factors —

* Institutional factors such as traffic mix, gauge-mix, topography, working habits of people etc. Such factors change only over a long period of time; and

* Efficinecy factors such as structure and use of assets, under capitalisation, over capitalisation, etc.

If the institutional factors of two railways are the same, or if we can treat the institutional factors as constant or somehow incorporate the impact of institutional factors into the capital output ratios, then the productivity of capital and efficiency of capital would imply the same thing. And then the difference in the capital output ratios of two railways can be legitimately compared and be said to be the result of differences in efficiency factors alone. It is important to make this distinction because except in very long run or in exceptional circumstances as the recent massive gauge conversion program of Indian Railways, in the normal course it is only the efficiency factors which can be controlled not the institutional factors.

However, since the institutional factors of two railways are in actual practice not the same they cannot be treated as a constant. The only way, therefore, is to incorporate the impact of the institutional factors in the capital output ratio so that it represents both the productivity as well as the efficiency factors. This may be done by indexing both output and capital in the current year to output and capital in a base year. Since the same set of institutional factors would be operating in the current year as well as the base year (provided the time gap between the two is not very large or the institutional factors are not artificially disturbed like the recent gauge conversion program), by indexing the output and capital in the current year to those in the base year the effect of the institutional factors can be said to get incorporated into the index. The difference between the productivities in the two years can then be said to be the result of efficiency factors only. A comparison of productivity ratios of two railways would reflect the differences in efficiecy of capital.

It then follows that although it may not be justified to expect that if Rs.100.00 invested in railway A leads to an increase of 50 TUs in railway A, then the same should happen on railway B; it may be reasonable to say that if 10 % increase in capital of Railway A leads to 3% increase in its TUs, and a similar ratio prevails on Railway B then the productivity and efficiency of capital use on the two railways is the same. This is the essence of the alternative approach, which is an indexed approach to measuring productivity of capital.

In this approach investment and output in a particular year are indexed to investment and output in a base year. And productivity is defined as a ratio of the two indices.

Thus, two more concepts of capial output ratio emerge.

a) Indexed Average Capital Output Ratio (INDCOR)

The INDCOR for current year may be defined as

$$\text{INDCOR} = \frac{\left(\dfrac{BT + IT}{BT}\right) 100}{\left(\dfrac{BC + IC}{BC}\right) 100}$$

$$= \frac{BT + IT}{BT} \times \frac{BC}{BC + IC}$$

$$= \frac{BC}{BT} \times \frac{BT + IT}{BC + IC}$$

$$= \frac{1}{\text{ACOR in Base Year}} \times \text{ACOR in Current Year}$$

$$= \frac{\text{ACOR in Current Year}}{\text{ACOR in Base Year}}$$

This is like ACOR of the conventional concept.

b) Indexed Incremental Capital Output Ratio (INDICOR)

The INDICOR for current year may be defined as

$$\text{INDICOR} = \frac{\frac{IT}{BT} \times 100}{\frac{IC}{BC} \times 100}$$

$$= \frac{IT}{BT} \times \frac{BC}{IC}$$

$$= \frac{BC}{BT} \times \frac{IT}{IC}$$

$$= \frac{\text{ICOR in Current Year}}{\text{ACOR in Base Year}}$$

This is akin to ICOR in conventional concept, as the incremental element only is being considered.

The following points emerge from the above definitions -

i) It will be seen that both INDCOR and INDICOR are inversely related to ACOR in the base year. This means that if in the current year two railways have the same ACOR or ICOR, then the railway having higher ACOR in Base Year will have lower INDCOR or INDICOR in the curerent year and vice versa. This stands to reason. For, it implies that the railway having lower productivity of capital earlier has been able to improve its capital utilisation.

For example if in the current year INDICOR of A > INDICOR of B, then according to the above expressions:

$$\frac{\text{ICOR of A}}{\text{ACOR of A in Base Year}} > \frac{\text{ICOR of B}}{\text{ACOR of B in Base Year}}$$

However, if in the current year ICOR of A = ICOR of B then the above expression can hold true only if ACOR of A in Base Year < ACOR of B in Base Year. This implies that in the current year (although ICORs of the two railways are the same) railway A has become more capital productive than railway B.

It is important to note that if conventional ICOR approach is adopted, the equality of ICOR of the two railways places them on the same footing. Whereas, if the indexed approach is adopted, the fact of improvement in capital utilisation of railway A is also brought out and the two railways even though having the same ICOR in the current year, do not remain on the same footing.

This is another important reason why the indexed approach to the evaluation of capital output ratio can be said to have a definite edge over the conventional definition. It is more realistic and more logical. Therefore, for evaluation of capital productivity in different zonal railways the indexed approach is more relevant than the conventional approach.

ii) It is obvious that INDCOR and INDICOR would give different values and extent of difference between the two would be

$$= \text{INDCOR} - \text{INDICOR}$$

$$= \left(\frac{BC}{BT} \times \frac{BT+IT}{BC+IC} \right) - \left(\frac{BC}{BT} \times \frac{IT}{IC} \right)$$

$$= \frac{BC}{BT} \left(\frac{BT+IT}{BC+IC} - \frac{IT}{IC} \right)$$

$$= \frac{BC}{BT} \left(\frac{IC \,.\, BT - IT.BC}{IC^2 + IC.BC} \right)$$

While the absolute value of the difference between INDCOR and INDICOR is given by the above expression, which of the two would be greater will be given by the values of (IC.BT) and (IT.BC).

INDICOR > INDCOR if IC.BT < IT.BC, and

INDICOR < INDCOR if IC.BT > IT.BC.

iii) Relationship between INDICOR and INDCOR may also be expressed in another way.

Assume that in the current year -

INDICOR > INDCOR

$$= \frac{IT}{BT} \times \frac{BC}{IC} > \frac{BC}{BT} \times \frac{BT + IT}{BC + IC}$$

$$= \frac{BC}{BT} \times \frac{IT}{IC} > \frac{BC}{BT} \times \frac{BT + IT}{BC + IC}$$

$$= \frac{IT}{IC} > \frac{BT + IT}{BC + IC}$$

or ICOR > ACOR

Which means that INDICOR > INDCOR if ICOR > ACOR and vice versa. From the Annexures it will be seen that INDICOR is always less than INDCOR. This is because surprisingly ICOR has always been less than ACOR as may be seen in Table 1 though it need not necessarily always be so. There is no inherent reason why ICOR should necessarily be less than ACOR. In fact, it should generally be the other way round for better productivity. One plausible reason for ICOR more or less consistently being less than ACOR could be that in this study investments have not been revalued to any base year. If they are, the revalued incremental investments would definitely turn out to be less than their face value. This would give a better ICOR. What would then be the relationship between ICOR and ACOR is difficult to predict.

Thus, two non-conventional definition of Capital Output ratios have emerged - INDCOR and INDICOR. Of these, INDICOR is preferable because it is based on the concept of marginal productivity as against INDCOR which is like average productivity.

Evaluating Productivity

After computing the capital output ratios - whether according to the conventional method or the Indexed method - it is necessary to evaluate the ratios. Two types of evaluations are necessary. One, an inter-railway comparison to decide which railway is more productive. But this alone is not adequate. Railway A may be more productive than railway B, but still Railway A may not be productive enough in the sense that it may be employing more capital than really required. Therefore, the second kind of evaluation becomes necessary i.e. to find out whether the ratio represents a good or bad productivity. Obviously, this requires a comparison with some kind of a standard. Unfortunately, no standards regarding productivity exist except perhaps the cut off rate of return announced by Ministry of Railways from time to time for evaluating the productivity of individual projects.

But this is at the micro level and need not necessarily be so at the macro level. At the macro level the only criteria at present is the ratio of Net Revenue to capital-at-charge. The inadequacy of this ratio has already been established.

Thus, for want of anything better, it is suggested that the Indian Railway average of capital output ratio may be adopted as the minimum which a zonal railway must attempt to achieve. This is not to say that the IR average is the ideal or the best achievable result. It only means that the IR Average is the minimum which a railway must achieve. If this happens, over a period of time the IR Average will also increase as improvement in the productivity of railways having lower capital output ratios will automatically push up the average. This will have a very healthy trend on capital productivity. The IR Average may therefore be adopted as the minimum standard. This standard may be made more liberal by a weightage factor say ± 10% or so within which all railways must fall for IR productivity to be maximised.

Two statements regarding investments and productivity need to be made :

Investments on a railway may be considered

HIGH (H) if $P > Q (1 + x/100)$

EQUAL (E) if $Q (1 + x/100) > P > Q (1 - x/100)$

LOW (L) if $P < Q (1- x/100)$

Where

P is ratio of that railway's investment to total IR investment during the period.

Q is ratio of that railway's TU to total IR TU at the beginning of the period.

x is the weightage factor.

Similarly, Productivity on a railway may be considered

HIGH (H) if $A > B (1 + x/100)$

EQUAL (E) if $B (1 + x/100) > A > B (1 - x/100)$

LOW (L) if $A < B (1 - x/100)$

Where

A is Capital Output Ratio of the zonal railway

B is IR Average

x is weightage factor

x is a weightage factor or a tolerance both for investment share and productivity such that a deviation to this extent from the standard may be considered as normal. In this study an uniform weightage factor of 10% has been adopted for both. A different percentage may be adopted. In fact even different percentages for investment share and productivity may also be adopted. A very liberal weightage factor, however, would render the whole exercise meaningless.

The above is applicable to all four concepts of productivity of capital.

Throughout this study, the words HIGH, LOW and EQUAL have been used in the above sense.

In this study a relationship between Investment levels at the beginning of a period and the productivity levels at the end of a period has been analysed to see whether a zonal railway's investments share being HIGH, EQUAL or LOW has any relationship to its productivity being HIGH, EQUAL or LOW at the end of the period. This relationship is being analysed at the beginning and at the end of a period of time rather than in the same year because if such an inter-period relationship exists it can be used for future resource allocation purposes. To explain further, it is possible to establish a relationship between Investment share in 1991 and Productivity in 1991 itself but apart from it being a purely statistical relationship (as it would not be recognising the phenomenon of time lag between investment and output) such a relationship would not be of much practical use. It will not help to determine in 1994 what should be the resource allocaion in 1995 because the TU share of the railway in 1995 is not known in 1994. Whereas if a relationship between Investment share say in 1984 and Productivity in 1990 can be established then TU shares of different railways at the present point of time may be used to determine its resouce allocation in future years so that productivities of all railways are maximised.

The above discussion forms the basis for the analysis in the subsequent chapters.

5

The Unexplained Phenomenon

HAVING established the conceptual framework of capital productivity in the context of Indian Railways, it is now pertinent to examine the productivity of capital in different railway zones. Overcapitalisation and under capitalisation both are undesirable. Overcapitalisation is wasteful. There are innumerable examples of overcapitalisation - procurement of equipment of much larger capacity than actually required, excessive expenditure on model stations as done during 1985-90, airconditioning of computerised reservation offices in non-essential areas are just a few. Similarly, undercapitalisation affects output e.g. inadequate loading/un-loading facilities for block rakes at terminals, antiquated signalling and telecom facilities, capital starved suburban railway systems etc.

One way of examining whether there has been overcapitalisation is to examine the capital output ratios of different railways. According to the theory of economics, optimum deployment of capital is obtained when the Marginal Productivity of capital is equal in all its alternative uses. This presumes perfect divisibility and mobility of capital. Existence of imperfections would lead to deviation from the optimum. We can rephrase the above law to say that the optimum deployment of capital on zonal railways is obtained when the

Marginal Productivity of capital on all the railways is the same. The following points in this context need further clarification.

* Marginal Productivity and capital output ratio do not strictly mean the same thing. The former presumes that other factors of production are constant, whereas no such assumption is necessary for capital output ratio. Still the above law of economics applies equally well to capital output ratio also.

* A relationship between investment and output can be relevant only if investment is for output. Actually in railways, as anywhere else, not all investments are for output. This question has already been discussed in Chapter 3.

* As regards the existence of 'imperfections' the difference between institutional factors of individual railways has already been recognised, and that is why a different definition of output capital ratio has been adopted. However, the impact of two of the most important institutional factors viz. traffic mix and gauge-mix have been further examined in this Chapter.

Let us now have a look at the capital output ratios of Average Total Investment and Average Total Traffic Units for the period 1988-89 to 1992-93 for the zonal railways, calculated on the basis of all the four concepts - ACOR, ICOR, INDCOR and INDICOR. The terms Average Total Investment and Average Traffic Unit are explained later but for the moment it may suffice to say that these indicate the average of investments and traffic units during a period of time. Results shown in Table 2 have been extracted from Annexure-25.

Table 2

Productivity of Average Total Investment 1988-89/92-93

ACOR *92-93*		*ICOR* *88-89/92-93*		*INDCOR* *88-89/92-93*		*INDICOR* *88-89/92-93*	
WR	1.209	CR	0.516	CR	0.899	CR	0.389
CR	1.191	SE	0.370	ER	0.881	SE	0.342
NR	1.018	SC	0.289	SE	0.881	ER	0.277
SC	0.957	ER	0.255	WR	0.875	SC	0.262
SE	0.952	NE	0.207	NF	0.880	NF	0.252
NE	0.872	WR	0.186	SC	0.857	NE	0.200
ER	0.809	NF	0.137	NE	0.844	WR	0.134
SR	0.595	NR	0.136	SR	0.820	SR	0.136
NF	0.479	SR	0.097	NR	0.812	NR	0.108
IR	0.944	IR	0.257	IR	0.860	IR	0.234

Irrespective of the definition of capital output ratio, the wide inter-railway differences and also their difference with IR Average may be noticed. Optimally, each of them should have been equal to or within a narrow range of IR Average. The extent of difference from IR Average shows the deviation from optimum.

Why has this happened ?

Had the above comparisons been based only on the conventional concepts of capital productivity viz. ACOR and ICOR it would have been possible to state that the differences are because of differences in the institutional factors of different railways. But the comparison is based on the indexed approaches also viz. INDCOR and INDICOR which is supposed to have taken into account inter-railway differences of institutional factors. Then, why has it so happened ?

Two reasons, which are a part of the institutional factors, are often cited - traffic mix and gauge mix. A railway having larger proportion of its traffic in the form of freight traffic rather than passenger traffic is believed to produce more traffic units per unit of investment as compared to a passenger oriented railway. Similarly, a BG system is considered more capital productive than a MG system. It would be of interest to examine the effect of these two of the most important institutional factors.

The traffic-mix and gauge-mix of different zonal railways for the year 1992-93 is given below.

Table 3

Traffic-mix and Gauge-mix 1992-93

Rly.	*NTKM(M)*	*PKM(M)*	*% PKM Total*	*ETKM BG*	*ETKM MG+NG*	*%MG+NG Total*	*Op.Ratio %*
CR	41383	28523	40.81	19224	766	3.83	76.5
ER	26966	13445	33.27	16593	134	0.80	98.4
NR	41532	23458	36.09	15968	3730	18.94	86.5
NE	6928	11259	61.91	1560	5605	78.23	182.7
NF	6299	3381	34.93	1726	5151	74.90	187.9
SR	13622	11641	46.08	7036	4843	40.77	118.5
SC	26325	12883	32.86	10512	4197	28.53	85.8
SE	54558	6898	11.22	20742	1795	7.96	69.0
WR	34777	23453	40.28	10356	7583	42.27	70.9
IR	252388	134945	34.84	103717	33804	24.58	87.4

Effect of Traffic-Mix

Traffic-mix is normally expected to have a direct impact on capital productivity. It is the general belief that a freight oriented railway yields more output per unit of capital. The result obtained for the period 1988-89/92-93 is tabulated below.

Table 4

Traffic-mix and Productivity of Av. Total Investment 1992-93

Tfc.Mix	*ACOR*	*ICOR*	*INDCOR*	*INDICOR*	*Produc. Score*	*Ranking*
1	2	3	4	5	6	7
11.22 SE 1	4	2	2	2	10	2
32.86 SC 2	5	3	6	4	18	4
33.27 ER 3	7	4	2	3	16	3
34.93 NF 4	9	7	4	5	25	7
36.09 NR 5	3	8	9	9	28	8
40.28 WR 6	1	6	5	7	19	5
40.81 CR 7	2	1	1	1	5	1
46.08 SR 8	8	9	8	7	32	9
61.91 NE 9	6	5	7	6	24	6

In Col.1, the name of the railway and its ranking in Traffic Mix has been shown in descending order i.e. smaller proportion of PKM and larger proportion of NTKM is considered more favourable hence ranked higher. Besides rank, the ratio of PKM to Total TU has also been shown. Thus 11.22 SE 1 means that the ratio of PKM to Total TU on SE is 11.22 and it has the ranking of 1. See Table 3 above.

In other columns viz. 2, 3, 4 & 5 the Productivity ranking of the railways indicated in Col.1 is shown. For example, 2 in Col.3 against SE means that SE railway had second ranking in productivity according to the ICOR method and so on. See Annexure-25.

Obviously, productivity ranking of 1 is the most preferable situation. Thus a Productivity Score of 4 means a ranking of 1 under each method and is the lowest possible score. Col.6 shows the sum total of rankings in the four methods and thus is the Productivity Score for each railway. The lowest score is the most preferable situation. It needs to be emphasised that the Productivity Score is for all the four concepts of capital productivity put together. Hence, no bias in favour of any method is shown.

Col.7 shows the ranking of railways according to Productivity Score.

We may now see the ranking of the railways according to Traffic Mix in juxtaposition with ranking according to Productivity Score.

Table 5

Traffic Mix and Productivity Score 1992-93

	Traffic Mix		*Productivity Score*	
Railway	*Ratio %*	*Rank*	*Score*	*Rank*
SE	11.22	1	10	2
SC	32.86	2	18	4
ER	33.27	3	16	3
NF	34.93	4	25	7
NR	36.07	5	28	8
WR	40.28	6	19	5
CR	40.81	7	5	1
SR	46.08	8	32	9
NE	61.91	9	24	6

The following points may be noted.

* SE railway decidedly has a very favourable traffic mix. In fact, its advantage in traffic mix is overwhelming. Given this advantage, its Productivity Score should have been the best. But it is not so.

* The best Productivity Score is of CR which has the third worst traffic mix.

* NE railway has the worst traffic mix. Actually, traffic-mix is very adversely weighted against that railway, but its Productivity Score ranking is sixth. And in terms of absolute numbers while SR has Traffic-mix of 46.08 and Productivity Score 32, NE has Traffic-mix

of 61.91 which is much worse than on SR and Productivity Score of 24 which is much better than on SR.

* Although the Traffic-mix of SC, ER and NF are very close to each other their Productivity Scores vary from 16 to 25.

Therefore, it would be quite logical to conclude that Traffic-mix does not have much relationship with capital productivity. This, of course, is against commonly accepted belief.

Effect of Gauge-mix

Effect of gauge-mix on capital productivity can be analysed on similar lines.

Table 6

Gauge-mix and Productivity of Av. Total Investments 1992-93

Gauge.Mix	*ACOR*	*ICOR*	*INDCOR*	*INDICOR*	*Produc. Score*	*Ranking*
1	2	3	4	5	6	7
0.80 ER 1	7	4	2	3	16	3
3.83 CR 2	2	1	1	1	5	1
7.96 SE 3	4	2	3	1	10	2
18.94 NR 4	3	7	9	9	28	8
28.53 SC 5	5	3	6	4	18	4
40.77 SR 6	8	9	8	7	32	9
42.27 WR 7	1	6	5	7	19	5
74.90 NF 8	9	7	4	5	25	7
78.23 NE 9	6	5	7	6	24	6

As in the case of Table 4 dealing with Traffic-mix Col.1 above shows ranking of railways in the descending order of favourable gauge-mix. Thus 7.96 SE 3 means that on SE railway the ratio of MG+NG ETKM to Total ETKM is 7.96 and the railway is ranked third best on this criteria. Other columns mean the same as in the previous Table.

The ranking of railways based on Gauge-mix and Productivity Score would thus be as under :

Table 7

Gauge-Mix and Productivity Score 1992-93

	Gauge-Mix		*Productivity Score*	
Railway	*Ratio*	*Rank*	*Score*	*Rank*
ER	0.80	1	16	3
CR	3.83	2	5	1
SE	7.46	3	10	2
NR	18.94	4	28	8
SC	28.53	5	18	4
SR	40.77	6	32	9
WR	42.27	7	19	5
NF	74.90	8	25	7
NE	78.23	9	24	6

The following points need to be noted.

* ER has overwhelmingly favourable Gauge-mix but it is third in Productivity Score.
* The Gauge-mix on CR is very favourable and it also ranks first in productivity.
* The ranking of SE is third in respect of Gauge-mix and second in respect of productivity.

Thus the first three railways in Gauge-mix have the first three positions in productivity also. This perhaps is one of the arguments in favour of large scale gauge conversion work taken up by Indian Railways during the last three or four years.

But beyond this the story is quite different.

* ER with Gauge-mix of 0.80 has Productivity Score of 16 where as CR with Gauge-mix of 3.83 has Productivity Score of 5. Actually, it should have been the other way round.

* WR and SR are more or less similar in Gauge-mix but while WR has Productivity Score of 19, that of SR is 32.

* Gauge-mix on NF and NE is much worse than on SR but Productivity Score of both is much better than on SR.

* If gauge-mix had an effect on capital productivity ER should have been the most productive and NE the least productive railways because the gauge-mix on both are not only relatively the best and the worst but absolute value-wise also while ER is very good NE has an extremely unfavourable mix. But in actual fact, this is not so. Neither ER has the best nor NE the worst Productivity Score.

In view of the above, it would be erroneous to say that gauge by itself has a direct bearing on the capital productivity of railways. This by no means can be construed as an argument for or against the current emphasis on gauge conversion on Indian Railways. In all fairness, the question of gauge conversion may have to be looked at from many other angles. But from the point of capital productivity the above evidence does suggest that there is no direct identifiable relationship between gauge-mix and capital productivity.

It can thus be seen that the conventional beliefs regarding the effect of traffic-mix and gauge-mix on productivity of capital are not borne out by actual data.

Effect of Non-economic Considerations

Another factor which could affect the productivity of capital is investments made on other than purely economic considerations. It is a fact that railways have to make some investments based on purely non-economic considerations such as - for development of underdeveloped areas, social benefit, welfare, public image and even political considerations. But quite often much is made of this factor.

There are no statistics to show how much of railway's investment decisions were made on non-economic considerations. Apart from inadvisability of maintaining such data, there are practical constraints as well. For example, it is not uncommon to inflate earnings and deflate cost estimates of projects to make uneconomic projects appear profitable so that they can be said to have been selected for investment purely on economic consideration. This being so, it is not possible to find out which projects were selected on non-economic considerations.

However, if we look at the structure of railway investments - reasonably well represented by the structure of the Plan Heads- it will be seen that very few of the Plan Heads are such which can be said to attract non-economic considerations or outside influences. It is difficult to put any percentages, but it is felt that barring aberrations in individual years, over a period of time not more than 5% of investments can be said to have been made on non-economic or extraneous considerations.

Even if there are some investment decisions based on non-economic considerations, the basic conclusions of this study are not materially vitiated. This is because it can be assumed that over a period of time the extent of non-economic investment decisions in all the railways would be more or less the same. Hence inter-railway comparisons and ranking of railways according to capital productivity as done in this study can still be safely done.

Micro and Macro

The foregoing discussion shows that whatever definition of capital output ratio one adopts, the capital output ratios of various zonal railways are widely divergent. This divergence cannot be explained away by differences in traffic-mix and gauge-mix or by investments based on non-economic considerations alone. Therefore one must look for the reasons for these differences some where else.

Could it be that the reasons for the difference lie in the planning, investment decision and resource allocation processes themselves rather than anything else ?

Indian railways do have a planning process and investment policies. There is a system of making Corporate Plan which is translated into Five Year Plans and Annual Plans. Well known project formulation, evaluation, selection and management techniques have been adopted in varying degrees. Guidelines have also been laid down in various orders and circulars. In spite of this, wide inter-railway differences in capital productivity do exist which affect the productivity of Indian Railways as a whole.

One reason for inter-railway differences in productivity perhaps could be errors at any of the stages of the project life, most important being errors in estimating due to one reason or the other. But then some error in estimating costs and benefits will always remain in spite of the best techniques adopted.

Therefore, in addition to improving techniques of estimating, project selection and management and in addition to the plans, policies and appraisal techniques already existing, the question naturally arises whether this is adequate or whether something more needs to be done. Is there a missing link ? Raising only the cut off rate for project selection, presently 14%, is obviously no solution.

It is felt that for reasons for the situation described above, one must look into the planning and investment decision process itself.

* The process is characterised by what may be called the micro-approach. Each investment proposal is looked at in isolation. The impact of the sum total of all investments on the system as a whole is hardly ever assessed or evaluated.

* The micro-approach also is not taken to its logical conclusions. A comprehensive logical micro approach would require that - each investment proposal be listed

and arranged in the descending order of its projected rate of return with the cost indicated against each. Needless to say the list would include only those projects which yield at least the cut off rate. Then all those projects the cumulative cost of which equal the available funds should be selected and others rejected. Further, refinements to take care of on-going projects as well as new projects would also have to be provided. However, at present no such mechanism exists. Actually, having such a mechanism is neither desirable nor practicable for a vast organisation like Indian Railways where the list of projects in any year, both new and on-going, is rather stupendous.

Thus, while on the one hand a micro-approach has been adopted, on the other it has not, indeed cannot, be taken to its logical conclusions.

* The suceptibility of the micro approach to too much subjectivity has already been discussed e.g. artificially inflating earning estimates and deflating cost estimates.

* At present it is possible for more than one project, which actually should be sub-projects of a project, to take advantage of the same "projected benefits" and meet the cut off rate when considered individually, but fail to do so if the costs and benefits of all such sub-projects are taken together. Although instructions exist to guard against such a situation, there is no mechanism to ensure that this does not happen particularly if the works are on two different Divisions or railways.

A micro approach is therefore not adequate. It ought to be supplemented with a macro approach i.e. consideration of the impact of sum total of all investments on the total productivity of the system.

The micro analysis would identify the projects which meet the rate of return criteria and hence may be considered for implementation. The macro criteria would determine the sum total of the projects which should actually be selected. The macro criteria could in a way be the enveloping criteria within which sum total of all the projects must remain. In order to remain within the macro criteria, the individual projects may if necessary, either not be taken up at all or modified, as it is possible to have many alternative capital structures to obtain the same level of output. For example, there are more than one ways of obtaining the same level of line capacity, or obtain the same throughput.

At present, no such macro criteria exists. It is suggested that the volume of output of a railway represented by its Traffic Units may form the basis for such a macro criteria.

Firstly, it is much more objective in the sense that it is not based on any estimates hence not susceptible to subjectivity. Traffic Units are based on actual published statistics.

Secondly, as shown in this study, a relationship between the traffic units of a railway, its investments and its capital productivity does actually exist. And this relationship can be used to formulate a macro criteria for resource allocation.

The next three Chapters are devoted to exploring this relationship.

A hypothesis about the relationship is first made, that investments on a railway as a ratio of total investments on IR should not be higher than the ratio of its traffic units to total traffic units of IR over a period of time, otherwise the effect on capital productivity will be very adverse. This hypothesis is tested in the next three Chapters by adopting many different scenarios. After the hypothesis is established, its policy implications are discussed in the last Chapter.

6

Capital-at-Charge

As stated earlier, the main hypothesis of this study is that best results on capital productivity are obtained when investments on a railway are not higher than the ratio of its output to total output of IR. This hypothesis is being tested in this and the next Chapter.

It has been explained in Chapter-2 that investments on IR are financed from two sources - external resource from Govt. of India which is called capital-at-charge and internal resources. In this Chapter capital-at-charge only has been evaluated. In the next Chapter the total investment including capital-at-charge has been discussed.

In this Chapter the discussion is for two time periods viz. period 1970-71 to 1988-89 and 1988-89 to 1992-93. The former period is dealt with in Section 1 and the latter in Section 2. The methodology adopted in Section 2 is also slightly different.

SECTION 1 : PERIOD 1970-71 TO 88-89

As explained earlier, period 1970-71 to 1988-89 has again been divided into two parts 1970-71 to 1980-81 and 1980-81 to 1988-89. Analysis for both the periods has been separately done. In addition, analysis for the full period 1970-71 to 1988-89 has also been done.

Further, although in Chapter-4 the Indexed Approach to Capital-Output Ratio has been shown to be superior and INDICOR has been stated to be the most appropriate method, analysis has been done for all the four approaches - ACOR, ICOR, INDCOR and INDICOR.

Base data are available in the Annexures. Wherever necessary, specific annexures have been referred to.

A. Average Capital Output Ratio (ACOR)

i) 1970-71 to 1980-81

In Annexure-14 investment share between 1970-71 and 80-81 and TU share in 1970-71 has been taken to calculate whether Investment share is HIGH, EQUAL or LOW. Similarly, ACORs of the zonal railways in 1980-81 has been calculated and placed in HIGH, EQUAL or LOW category in Annexure-18. A relationship between the two has been traced in Table 8 below.

Table 8

RLY.	*INV.SHARE*	*ACOR*
CR	E	H
ER	L	E
NR	L	H
NE	E	H
NF	E	L
SR	H	L
SC	H	E
SE	E	L
WR	E	H

See Annexures 14 & 18

Chart 1

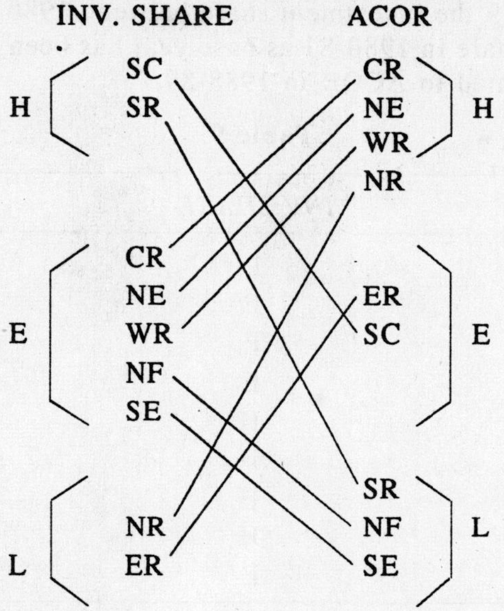

The relationship obtained in Table 8 has been clearly depicted in Chart 1. Following relationship may be seen -

a) Two HIGH investment shares led to one LOW productivity and one EQUAL productivity, or

1 L
2 H <
1 E

b) Five EQUAL investment shares led to three HIGH and two LOW productivities, or

3 H
5 E <
2 L

c) Two LOW investment shares led to one HIGH and one EQUAL productivities, or

1 H
2 L <
1 E

ii) 1980-81 to 88-89

In Table 9 the investment share between 1980-81 and 88-89 and TU share in 1980-81 as base year has been taken. This has been related to ACOR in 1988-89.

Table 9

RLY.	*INV.SHARE*	*ACOR*
CR	L	H
ER	E	E
NR	E	H
NE	E	E
NF	H	L
SR	H	L
SC	H	L
SE	H	L
WR	L	H

See Annexures 15 & 19

Chart 2

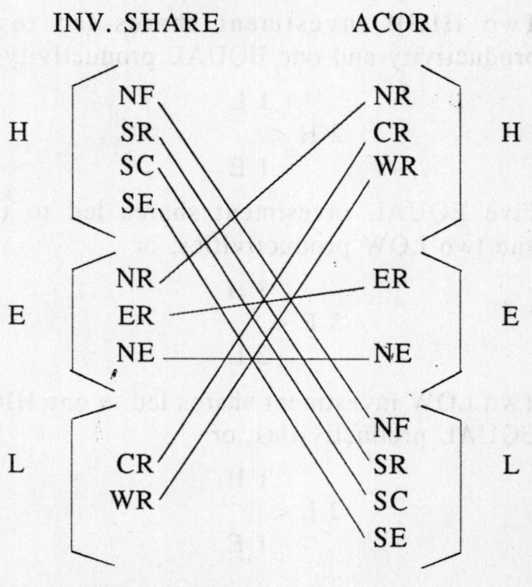

Chart 2 shows that -

a) Four HIGHs in investment share led to four LOWs in productivity, or

4 H — — — 4 L

b) Three EQUALs in investment share led to one HIGH and two EQUAL productivities, or

1 H
3 E <
2 E

c) Two LOWs in investment share led to two HIGHs in productivity, or

2 L — — — — 2 H

iii) 1970-71 to 1988-89

In Table 10, the overall period 1970-71 to 1988-89 has been taken.

Table 10

RLY.	*INV.SHARE*	*ACOR*
CR	E	H
ER	L	E
NR	E	H
NE	E	E
NF	H	L
SR	H	L
SC	H	L
SE	E	L
WR	L	H

See Annexures 16 and 20

Chart 3

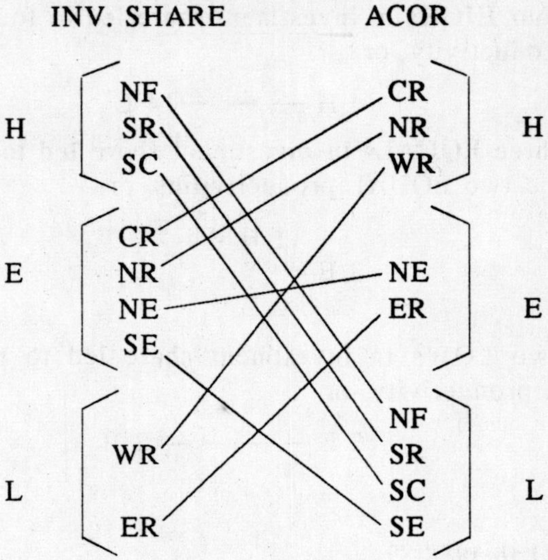

Chart 3 shows that -

a) Three HIGHs in investment share led to three LOWs in productivity, or

3 H ———— 3 L

b) Four EQUALs in investment share led to two HIGHs, one EQUALs and one LOW in productivity, or

2 H
4 E <— — 1 E
1 L

c) Two LOW in investment share led to one HIGH and one EQUAL productivity, or

1 H
2 L <
1 E

The above results are tabulated in Railway-wise Productivity Matrix for all the three periods in Table 11 below such that the first alphabet shows investment share and the second shows productivity. For example,

EH = EQUAL investment share and HIGH productivity.

Table 11

Railway-wise Productivity Matrix

	HH	*HE*	*HL*	*EH*	*EE*	*EL*	*LH*	*LE*	*LL*
CR				2			1		
ER					1			2	
NR				2			1		
NE				1	2				
NF			2			1			
SR			3						
SC		1	2						
SE			1			2			
WR				1			2		
	-	1	8	6	3	3	4	2	-

The following points are observed

a) SR always had HIGH investment share and LOW productivity.

b) SC & NF had twice (out of possible three times) HIGH investment and LOW productivity.

c) WR had twice LOW investment share and HIGH productivity.

d) Best results were obtained on CR and NR.

e) CR, ER, NR,NE and WR were never in HIGH investment category.

f) SE had HIGH investment share once and EQUAL investment share twice. It was in EQUAL investment share category for the overall period 1970-71 to 88-89. But it was always in the LOW productivity category.

g) NE was always in EQUAL investment share category, but in HIGH productivity category in 1970-71 to 80-81 and EQUAL productivity category in the period 80-81 to 88-89 and the overall period 1970-71 to 88-89.

h) CR and NR have always been in HIGH productivity category, although sometimes they have been in EQUAL and sometimes in LOW investment category.

The results obtained for the three periods can be tabulated in form of Productivity Matrix for all railways as shown in Table 12 below :

Table 12

Productivity Matrix

Investment Share		Productivity H	Productivity E	Productivity L
	H	-	1	8
Investment	E	6	3	3
Share	L	4	2	-

It will be seen that

a) HIGH investment share gives the worst result on productivity.

b) LOW investment share gives the best result.

c) EQUAL investment share has reasonably good impact on productivity.

d) If HIGH productivity is desired, investment share should in no case be HIGH. It could be EQUAL or LOW.

The above results have been obtained under the ACOR concept of productivity. Results under other concepts may differ.

B. Incremental Capital Output Ratio (ICOR)

Here the relationship between investment share and productivity of capital according to ICOR approach has been examined.

i) 1970-71 to 1980-81

In Table 13 investment share between 1970-71 and 80-81

and Incremental Capital Output Ratio between these two years has been taken.

Table 13

RLY.	*INV.SHARE*	*ICOR*
CR	E	H
ER	L	L
NR	L	H
NE	E	L
NF	E	L
SR	H	L
SC	H	L
SE	E	L
WR	E	H

See Annexures 14 & 18

Chart 4

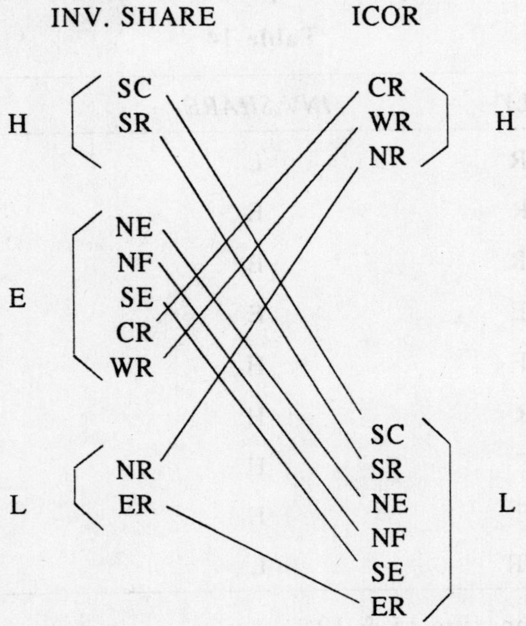

Chart 4 shows that -

a) Two HIGH investment shares led to two LOW productivities

2 H—— —2 L

b) Five EQUAL investment shares led to two HIGH and three LOW productivity,

2 H
5 E <
3 L

c) Two LOW investment shares led to one HIGH and one LOW productivity

1 H
2 L <
1 L

ii) 1980-81 to 1988-89

The relationship for this period is shown in Table 14.

Table 14

RLY.	*INV.SHARE*	*ICOR*
CR	L	E
ER	E	E
NR	E	H
NE	E	E
NF	H	L
SR	H	L
SC	H	L
SE	H	H
WR	L	H

See Annexure 15 & 19

Chart 5

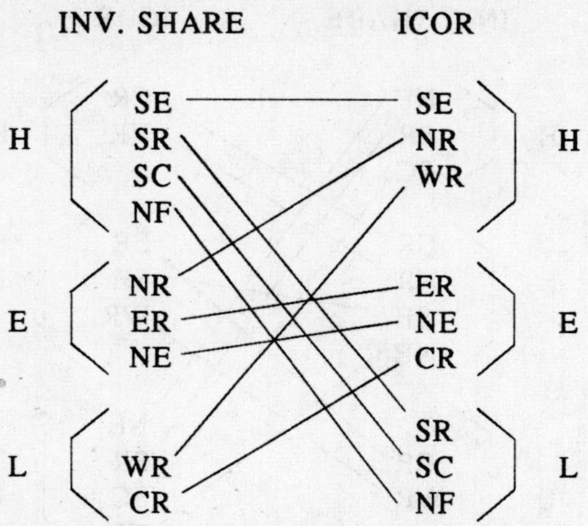

The following relationship emerges from Chart 5

4 H < 1 H, 3 L	3 E < 1 H, 2 E	2 L < 1 H, 1 E

iii) 1970-71 to 1988-89

For the overall period 1970-71 to 1988-89 the relationship is shown in Table 15.

Table 15

RLY.	*INV.SHARE*	*ICOR*
CR	E	H
ER	L	E
NR	E	H
NE	E	L
NF	H	L
SR	H	L
SC	H	L
SE	E	E
WR	L	E

See Annexures 16 & 20

Chart 6

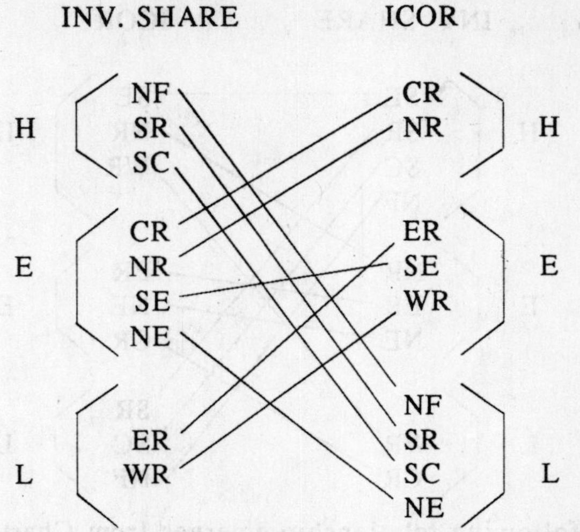

The relationship shown in Chart 6 gives the following results -

2 H

3 H — — 3 L   4 E <— — 1 E   2 L — 2 E

1 L

The above results are tabulated in a Railway-wise Productivity Matrix for all the three periods in Table 16 below:

Table 16

Railway-wise Productivity Matrix

	HH	*HE*	*HL*	*EH*	*EE*	*EL*	*LH*	*LE*	*LL*
CR				2				1	
ER					1			1	1
NR				2			1		
NE					1	2			
NF			2			1			
SR			3						
SC			3						
SE	1				1	1			
WR				1			1	1	
	1	-	8	5	3	4	2	3	1

The following points may be noted -

a) SC & SR always had HIGH investment share and LOW productivity.

b) Best results were obtained on NR. Under ACOR CR and NR had the same results (See Table 11). But under ICOR CR fell behind marginally which means that incremental capital was better utilised in NR than in CR.

c) Capital deployment in WR was better under ACOR than under ICOR. This means less productive use of incremental capital.

For all the three periods under ICOR the Investment Productivity Matrix for all railways is shown in Table 17

Table 17

Productivity Matrix

		Productivity		
		H	E	L
Investment Share	H	1	-	8
	E	5	3	4
	L	2	3	1

The Productivity Matrix in Table 17 leads to the following conclusions.

a) There is overwhelming evidence that HIGH investment share leads to LOW productivity.

b) If HIGH and EQUAL productivities are taken together, then best results are obtained when Investment share is EQUAL.

c) For HIGH productivity EQUAL investment share is most conducive.

So far the analysis has been done on the basis of the conventional definitions of capital output ratio. Analysis based on the Indexed approaches are given below.

C. Indexed Capital Output Ratio (INDCOR)

As explained earlier, in this approach the output and investment, both are indexed to output and investment in a base year and the capital output ratio is the ratio of the two indices.

The same three time periods have been taken for analysis.

i) 1970-71 to 1980-81

The relationship for this period is shown in Table 18.

Table 18

RLY.	*INV.SHARE*	*INDCOR*
CR	E	H
ER	L	E
NR	L	H
NE	E	L
NF	E	E
SR	H	L
SC	H	L
SE	E	L
WR	E	E

See Annexures 14 & 18

Chart 7

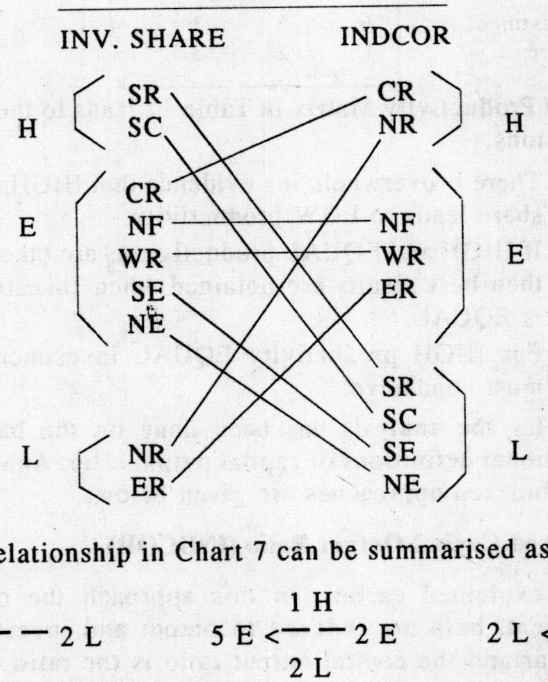

The relationship in Chart 7 can be summarised as under :

2 H —— 2 L

5 E < 1 H, 2 E, 2 L

2 L < 1 H, 1 E

It will be seen that HIGH investment share has not given any HIGH productivity. On the contrary, it has only given LOW productivity.

ii) 1980-81 to 1988-89

The relationship during this period is as shown below -

Table 19

RLY.	*INV.SHARE*	*INDCOR*
CR	L	E
ER	E	E
NR	E	E
NE	E	E
NF	H	E
SR	H	E
SC	H	L
SE	H	H
WR	L	E

See Annexures 15 & 19

Chart 8

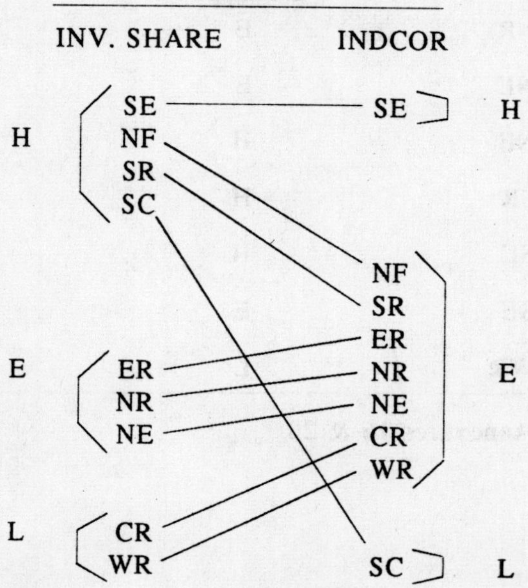

The relationship in Chart 8 may be summarised as under-

1 H
4 H< —— — 2 E , 3 E— —3 E , 2 L— —2 E
1 L

It may be noted that while EQUAL and LOW investment share produced EQUAL productivity, HIGH investment share mostly produced results of a lower category in productivity.

iii) 1970-71 to 1988-89

During the overall period 1970-71 to 88-89 the relationship given in Table 20 is found.

Table 20

RLY.	*INV.SHARE*	*INDCOR*
CR	E	H
ER	L	H
NR	E	H
NE	E	L
NF	H	L
SR	H	L
SC	H	L
SE	E	H
WR	L	E

See Annexures 16 & 20

Chart 9

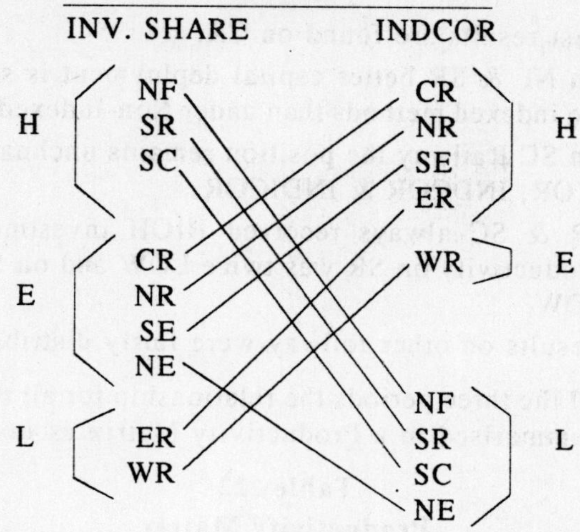

The relationship obtaining in Chart 9 shows that

3 H— —3 L   4 E < 3 H / 1 L   2 L < 1 H / 1 E

All the Railways having HIGH investment share had LOW productivity.

The above results are tabulated in a Railway-wise Productivity Matrix for all the three periods in Table 21 below:

Table 21
Railway-wise Productivity Matrix

	HH	*HE*	*HL*	*EH*	*EE*	*EL*	*LH*	*LE*	*LL*
CR				2				1	
ER					1		1	1	
NR				1	1		1		
NE					1	2			
NF		1	1		1				
SR		1	2						
SC			3						
SE	1			1		1			
WR					1			2	
	1	2	6	4	5	3	2	4	-

The following points may be noted -

a) Best results are found on CR.

b) On NF & SR better capital deployment is seen under the indexed methods than under Non-Indexed Methods.

c) On SC Railway the position remains unchnaged under ICOR, INDCOR & INDICOR.

d) SR & SC always received HIGH investment share. Productivity on SR was twice LOW and on SC always LOW.

e) Results on other railway were fairly distributed.

For all the three periods the relationship for all the railway may be summarised in a Productivity Matrix as in Table 22.

Table 22
Productivity Matrix

		Productivity		
		H	E	L
	H	1	2	6
Investment	E	4	5	3
Share	L	2	4	-

The following trends are seen from the above matrix :

a) In HIGH investment share category productivity was LOW in 66% cases.

b) In EQUAL investment share category most of the results obtained fell either in HIGH or EQUAL productivity category.

c) Best results were obtained in LOW investment category.

d) For HIGH productivity, EQUAL investment share is most conducive.

D. Indexed Incremental Capital Output Ratio (INDICOR)

As already explained, in the INDICOR approach only the incremental element of investment and output is taken for indexing and then the capital output ratio is calculated based on the two indices.

i) 1970-71 to 80-81

The relationship between investment share and INDICOR found during this period is given in Table 23.

Table 23

RLY.	*INV.SHARE*	*INDICOR*
CR	E	H
ER	L	L
NR	L	H
NE	E	L
NF	E	L
SR	H	L
SC	H	L
SE	E	L
WR	E	H

See Annexures 14 & 18

Chart 10

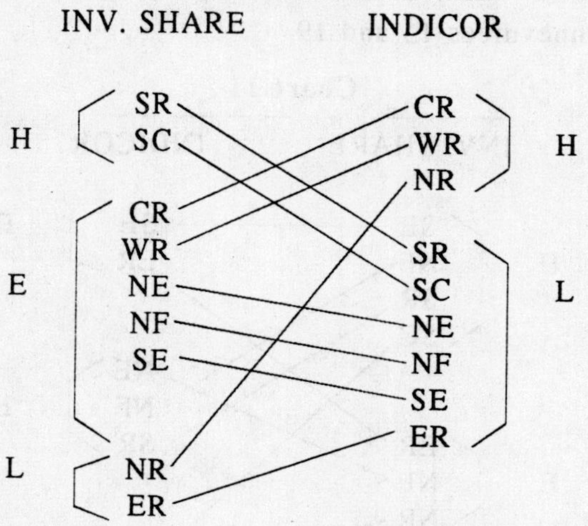

The following relationship emerges from Chart 10

2 H—— —2 L

5 E < 2 H, 3 L

2 L < 1 H, 1 L

All HIGH investments led to LOW productivities. Further, no HIGH productivity had HIGH investment also.

ii) 1980-81 to 88-89

The relationship found during this period is given in Table 24 below.

Table 24

RLY.	*INV.SHARE*	*INDICOR*
CR	L	L
ER	E	H
NR	E	L
NE	E	E
NF	H	E
SR	H	E
SC	H	L
SE	H	H
WR	L	L

See Annexurees 15 and 19

Chart 11

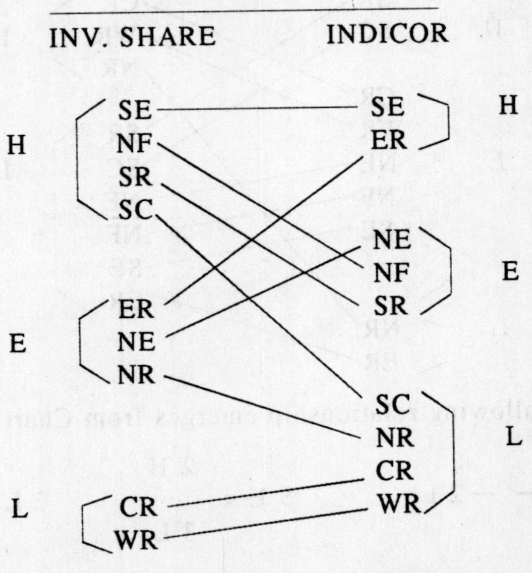

The relationship of Chart 11 may be summarised as under:

1 H 4 H<— — 2 E 1 L	1 H 3 E <— — 1 E 1 L	2 L— 2 L

Investment share and productivity both fell in the same category in case of LOW investment. Results were distributed in case of EQUAL investment share. And HIGH investment most of the time led to Productivity of lower category.

iii) 1970-71 to 88-89

For the overall period 1970-71 to 88-89 the following relationship is found in Table 25.

Table 25

RLY.	*INV.SHARE*	*INDICOR*
CR	E	H
ER	L	H
NR	E	H
NE	E	L
NF	H	E
SR	H	L
SC	H	L
SE	E	H
WR	L	L

See Annexures 16 and 20

Chart 12

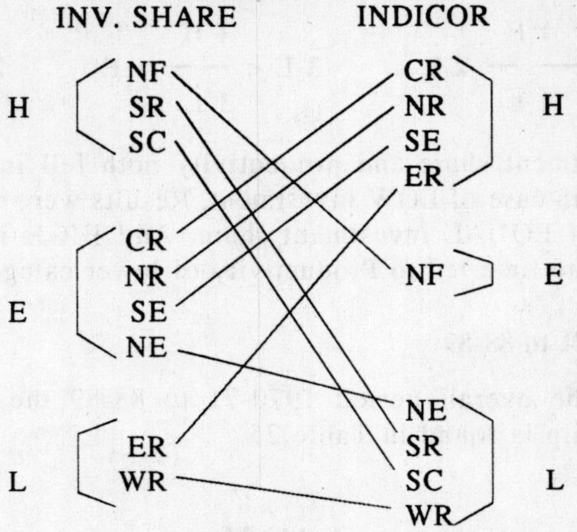

The relationship of Chart 12 can be summarised as under:

3 H < 1 E, 2 L	4 E < 3 H, 1 L	2 L < 1 H, 1 L

Here, in the overall period HIGH productivity is found only in case of EQUAL and LOW investment share and all HIGH investments led to productivity of a lower category.

The above results for the three periods are summarised in Railway-wise Productivity Matrix in Table 26.

Table 26

	HH	*HE*	*HL*	*EH*	*EE*	*EL*	*LH*	*LE*	*LL*
CR				2					1
ER				1			1		1
NR				1		1	1		
NE					1	2			
NF		2				1			
SR		1	2						
SC			3						
SE	1			1		1			
WR				1					2
	1	3	5	6	1	5	2	-	4

The following points may be noted -

a) Of all the occurrences of HIGH investment share only 10% yielded HIGH productivity and 55% yielded LOW productivity. On the other hand, of all the occurrences of EQUAL investment share, 50% yielded HIGH productivities and 40% yielded LOW productivitiy. And of all the occurrences of LOW investment share 30% yielded HIGH productivity and 70% LOW productivity.

b) Best results were obtained on CR.

c) SC always had HIGH investment but LOW productivity.

d) SR always had HIGH investment share but never HIGH productivity. Results in NF were better than in SR.

e) CR, ER, NR and NE never had HIGH investment share and the results on productivity were distributed but mostly tending towards HIGH productivity. In fact 50% of the time it was HIGH productivity and 60 % of the time it was HIGH plus EQUAL productivity.

f) HIGH investment share and HIGH productivity was very rare, it occurred only once out of a total of 27 occurrences.

A summarised Productivity Matrix for all the three periods and all the railways is given in Table 27.

Table 27

Productivity Matrix

		Productivity		
		H	E	L
	H	1	3	5
Investment	E	6	1	5
Share	L	2	-	4

The following conclusions may be drawn :

a) HIGH investment share and LOW investment share both led to mostly LOW productivity.

b) EQUAL investment share led to the best results on productivity

c) For HIGH productivity, EQUAL investment share is most conducive.

The results of the all the four methods and all the three time periods are now summarised and evaluated.

All Methods

A Railway-wise Productivity Matrix for all the four methods and all the three time periods is given in Table 28 below:

Table 28
Railway-wise Productivity Matrix

	HH	*HE*	*HL*	*EH*	*EE*	*EL*	*LH*	*LE*	*LL*
CR				8			1	2	1
ER				1	3		2	4	2
NR				6	1	1	4		
NE				1	5	6			
NF		3	5		1	3			
SR		2	10						
SC		1	11						
SE	3		1	2	1	5			
WR				3	1		3	3	2
	3	6	27	21	12	15	10	9	5

In the above table there are a total of 108 occurrences of investment share and productivity combination, each zonal railway having 12 combinations.

The following points may be noted -

a) SR and SC always had HIGH investment but they never had HIGH productivity. NF also had 66% times HIGH investment, but never HIGH productivity. It may also incidentally be mentioned that NF and SR have adverse operating ratio as well. Thus higher investment on these railways has neither led to better productivity of capital nor better operating ratio. But contrary to popular belief, Capital productivity on NF turns out to be better than even on SR and SC.

b) CR, ER,NR, NE and WR never had HIGH investment share and ER had LOW productivity twice and NR and CR had LOW productivity once and NE had 50% of the time LOW productivity. Of these five railways ER and NE have adverse operating ratio. NE did not have a bad record in capital productivity but has a very high operating ratio (Table 3).

c) NR turn out to have the best capital productivity with CR close behind.

d) It is difficult to escape the impression that NF, SR and SC are getting overcapitalised.

In Table 29 below the Productivity Matrix of all the four methods, all the periods and all the railways have been combined. This gives 108 occurrences of Investment Productivity combination.

Table 29

Productivity Matrix

		Productivity H	E	L	
	H	3	6	27	36
Investment	E	21	12	15	48
Share	L	10	9	5	24
		34	27	47	

The following trends emerge :

a) In HIGH investment share occurrences, not even 10% led to HIGH productivity. In approximately 75% of the cases it led to LOW productivity.

b) In EQUAL investment share occurrences, in about 44% cases HIGH Productivity resulted and in 68% cases HIGH plus EQUAL productivity resulted.

c) In cases of LOW investment share occurrences HIGH productivity resulted in about 40% cases and HIGH plus EQUAL productivity in 80 % of the cases.

d) For HIGH productivity it is better to have EQUAL investment share. Similarly for EQUAL productivity also it is better to have EQUAL investment share.

e) LOW productivity is decidedly likely to result if investment share is HIGH.

Thus for the period 1970-71 to 1988-89 certain very clear conclusions regarding the relationship between Investment share on a railway and productivity can be drawn.

SECTION 2: PERIOD 1988-89 TO 1992-93

As mentioned in the section on 'Methodology' in Chapter-3, a slightly different methodology for the period 1988-89 to 1992-93 has been followed. This is explained below.

In the analysis for the period 1970-71 to 1988-89, data for two years have been taken at a time for computation, e.g. 1970-71 and 1980-81 or 1980-81 and 1988-89. These are thus in a way snap shot pictures of two years. But it is possible that there might be freaks in those two years. For example, due to some reason unusually less freight may have been loaded in that particular year or heavy investments may have had to be made. These may lead to erroneous conclusions. In order to have reliable results, therefore, 'normal' years should be selected. But then it is almost impossible to say which years are 'normal' - free from floods, draughts, agitations etc. It would therefore be better to take averages of both traffic units and investments over a period of time hoping that, obeying the law of averages, the unusual occurrences would cancel out. Using averages is preferable from another point also. The ratios of traffic units and investment shares calculated on the basis of 'averages' can be actually used for resource allocation purposes. On the other hand the ratios calculated using so called 'normal' years may be too old for any practical use, if those 'normal' years happened to occur long time ago.

Analysis in this section is based on these averages. Traffic Units for each year from 1988-89 to 1992-93 have been added and averaged. The result has been taken as the Average Traffic Unit for 1988-89 as representative for the period 1988-89 to 1992-93. Another method could have been to take two years on either side of 1988-89. However, the method adopted here has been selected because it gives due consideration to latest figures available. The Average so arrived at becomes the base year data with respect to which data for 1992-93 have been evaluated. The same method has been adopted for investments also.

Average Traffic Unit calculations are at Annexure-11 and Average Capital-at-charge calculations are at Annexure-12. Investment share of the railways in relation to their traffic units are shown in Annexure-17 and productivity calculations are shown in Annexure-21. The relationship between investment share and capital productivity under the four concepts of capital output ratio are shown underneath.

A. Average Capital Output Ratio (ACOR)

The following relationship is found.

Table 30

RLY.	*INV.SHARE*	*ACOR*
CR	L	H
ER	L	E
NR	H	E
NE	E	E
NF	H	L
SR	H	L
SC	H	L
SE	E	E
WR	L	H

See Annexures 17 & 21

Chart 13

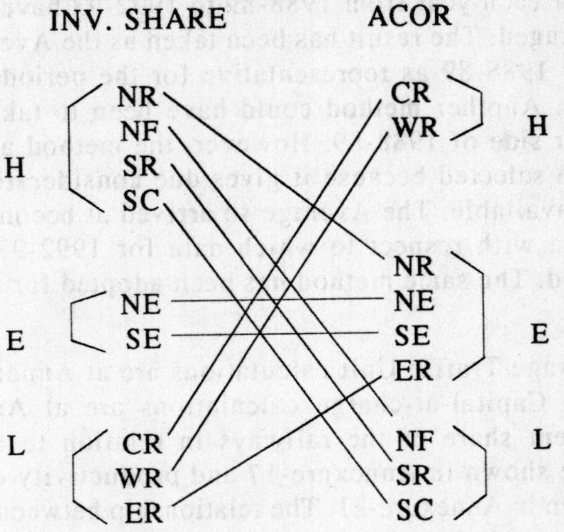

The relationship obtained in Table 30 is shown in Chart 13 which can be summarised as under

	E 1			H 2
H 4 <		E 2 — — E 2	L 3 <	
	L 3			E 1

B. Incremental Capital Output Ratio (ICOR)

The following relationship is found under ICOR.

Table 31

RLY.	*INV.SHARE*	*ICOR*
CR	L	H
ER	L	H
NR	H	H
NE	E	L
NF	H	L
SR	H	L
SC	H	L
SE	E	H
WR	L	L

See Annexures 17 & 21

Chart 14

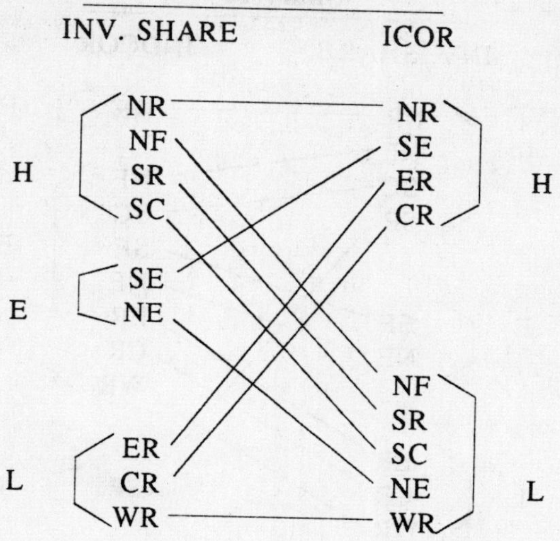

The relationship obtained in Table 31 has been shown in Chart 14. This can be summarised as under

H 4 < H 1 / L 3	E 2 < H 1 / L 1	L 3 < H 2 / L 1

C. Indexed Capital Output Ratio (INDCOR)

The following relationship is found under INDCOR.

Table 32

RLY.	*INV.SHARE*	*INDCOR*
CR	L	E
ER	L	E
NR	H	H
NE	E	E
NF	H	E
SR	H	L
SC	H	E
SE	E	E
WR	L	E

See Annexures 17 & 21

Chart 15

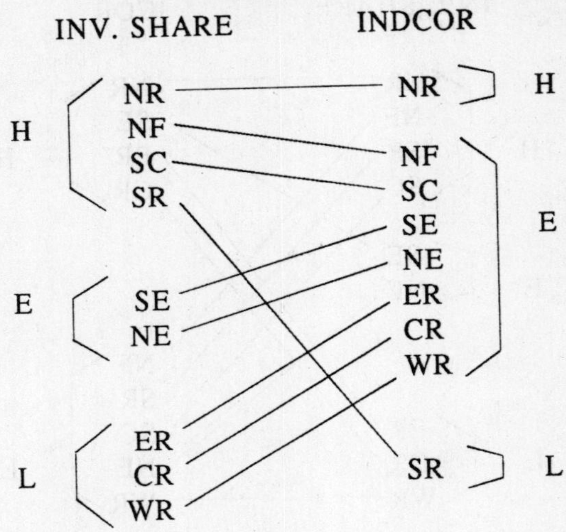

The relationship obtained in Table 32 has been shown in Chart 15. This can be summarised as under

H 1
H4 <— — E 2   E 2 — — E 2   L 3 —— E 3
L 1

D. Indexed Incremental Capital Output Ratio (INDICOR)

The following relationship has been found under INDICOR.

Table 33

RLY.	*INV.SHARE*	*INDICOR*
CR	L	E
ER	L	E
NR	H	H
NE	E	L
NF	H	L
SR	H	L
SC	H	L
SE	E	H
WR	L	L

See Annexures 17 & 21

Chart 16

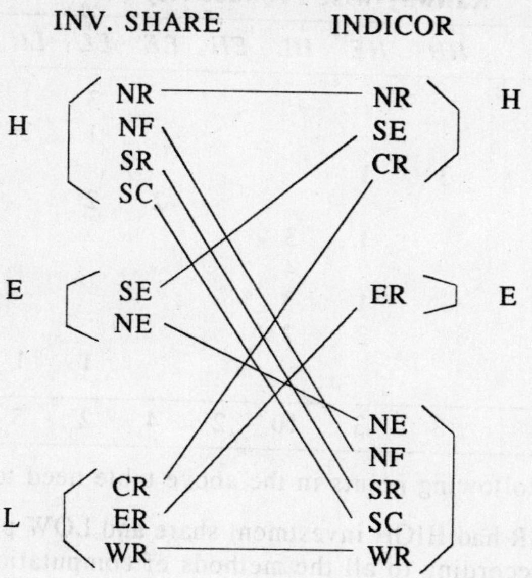

The relationship obtained in Table 33 has been shown in Chart 16. This can be summarised as under

	H 1		H 1		H 1
H 4 <		E 2 <		L 3 <	E 1
	L 3		L 1		L 1

Productivity Matrice

The results obtained in the four methods are tabulated further to get, irrespective of method - Railway-wise Productivity Matrix and then Productivity Matrix irrespective of method or railway.

Table 34
Railway-wise Productivity Matrix

	HH	*HE*	*HL*	*EH*	*EE*	*EL*	*LH*	*LE*	*LL*
CR						3	1		
ER						1	3		
NR	3	1							
NE					2	2			
NF		1	3						
SR			4						
SC		1	3						
SE		2	2						
WR						1	1	2	
Total	3	3	10	2	4	2	5	5	2

The following points in the above table need to be noted.

* SR had HIGH investment share and LOW productivity according to all the methods of computation.
* CR and ER had LOW investment share but three HIGH and one EQUAL productivity and one HIGH and three LOW productivities respectively.
* NF and SC had HIGH investment share and one EQUAL and three LOW productivity

As far as other railways are concerned there is nothing very striking about the results.

The Productivity Matrix irrespective of railway and method is given below.

Table 35
Productivity Matrix

		Productivity			
		H	E	L	
Investment Share	H	3	3	10	16
	E	2	4	2	8
	L	5	5	2	12
		10	12	14	

The following points may be noted.

* There are 16 occurrences of HIGH investment share. Of this 10 i.e. 63% resulted in LOW productivity and 19% in HIGH productivity.

* There are 12 occurrences of LOW investment share. Of these 5 or 42% resulted in HIGH prodctivity and another 42% in EQUAL productivity

* There are 10 occurrences of HIGH productivity. In only 30% of these cases investment share was also HIGH. In 70% cases, investment share was either EQUAL or LOW.

* There are 14 cases of LOW productivity. Of these 10 i.e. 71% had HIGH investment share and 14% LOW investment share. Both the LOW investment share and LOW productivity incidentally were on WR.

* Out of a total occurrence of 36 there are only 3 i.e. 8% cases where there are both HIGH investment share and HIGH productivity.

There is thus overwhelming evidence even based on Average Capital-at-charge and Average Traffic Units that HIGH investment share must be scrupulously avoided.

7

Total Investments

GRADUALLY the share of investments from loan capital as a ratio of Total Investments has been coming down. And since, output is the result of investments from internal resources also, it would not be correct to relate output to investments from capital only and end our analysis with discussion of capital-at-charge. The total investments from all sources should be examined.

Before analysing the investments from internal resources some clarifications are necessary. Amongst the internal resources, investments from Depreciation Reserve Fund are most important. During the period 1980-81 to 1992-93 investments from DRF formed 89.98% of investments from internal resources and 53.26% of Total Investments. During this period investments from DRF Rs.15313.12 crores outstripped investments from Capital Rs.11731.96 crores.

In this study all, or almost all, investments are being related to output. Sometimes, it is believed that DRF expenditure does not add to capacity. It only sustains the existing capacity, therefore it should not be related to creation of additional output. Before proceeding further, therefore, it is necessary to discuss the nature and effect of this kind of expenditure.

Discussion in this Chapter therefore, is divided into three parts. Section 1 deals with the general nature of Renewal and Replacement Expenses. Section 2 analyses the relationship between Investment share, Traffic Unit share and Productivity of Total Investments for the period 1980-81 to 1988-89. Period 1970-71 to 1980-81 has been ignored because of difficulty in getting the required data. In Section 3, the methodology has been slightly changed and period 1988-89 to 1992-93 discussed.

SECTION 1 : RENEWAL AND REPLACEMENT EXPENSES

It is generally believed that a renewal/replacement expenditure does not add to capacity. It only sustains the already existing capacity. Hence, DRF investments should not be related to output. But as would be seen from the rules for "Allocation of Expenditure" contained in Indian Railway Finance Code Volume I, this belief is not entirely correct. For example, as per Para 709 (5) all expenditure incurred on modernisation of Rolling Stock is borne by DRF. And modernisation of Rolling Stock does lead to capacity generation.

Further, even at a conceptual level renewals and replacements do lead to capacity generation. An asset is renewed or replaced when -

i) It is not performing i.e. it has become completely unusable.

ii) Performing at less than installed capacity and the installed capacity is still required.

iii) Higher capacity required.

iv) New assets would lead to reduced operating costs.

In the first three situations capacity additional to the existing one is bound to be created, howsoever small the addition be. Additional capacity is created even when the asset is replaced with an identical asset. For example, if an old coach is replaced with an identical new coach the availability of the coach for service increases due to lesser breakdowns, repairs and maintenance etc. and thus capacity additional to the one existing before replacement is created.

It may help to clarify matters if an asset is looked upon not as an asset but as a service.

It is important to realise that renewals and replacement expenditure does lead to capacity generation. And capacity generation should only be governed by the requirements of output. If the output level does not require the asset or the asset with a degraded level of performance is adequate to serve the need, there is no reason why the asset should be renewed or replaced. Therefore, it is quite logical to analyse renewals and replacement expenditure (and hence Total Investment) in relation to output.

But volume of output is only one of the determinants of renewals and replacement expenditure. Actually this expenditure would depend upon the following other factors -

a) Condition profile of the asset i.e. its age and use. Not much published data exists on the condition profile of assets on Indian Railways. But, for a given size and age profile of the capital base, the volume of output or in railway parlance the density of traffic may give a reasonably good idea of the condition profile of the assets. A railway with higher density of traffic would have more intensive use of its assets and therefore worse condition profile of asset and hence higher requirement of renwals and replacements.

b) Capital base. Given the same or similar condition profile, higher the capital base higher will be the requirement of renewals and replacements. It may be pointed out here that, in the context of railways, for purposes of renewals and replacement expenditure the capital base as shown in the Block Account - as distinguished from capital base as shown in Loan Account - is more relevant. The terms Loan Account and Block Account have been clarified in Annexure-1 : Glossary of Terms.

One inherent result of renewals and replacements should be fall in operating expenses (assuming constant prices of inputs) per unit of output. Thus on Railway A if greater proportion of its assets have been renewed or replaced as compared to Railway B, then operating expense per Traffic Unit on Railway A should be less than that on Railway B. But since constant prices cannot be assumed it would be quite adequate and also correct to say that its ratio of increase on Railway A should be less than the ratio of increase on Railway B.

Let us now see DRF expenditure on various zonal railways for the period 1980-81 to 1992-93 in relation to the above parameters.

DRF, Block Account and Operating Expenses

In Table 36 DRF expenditure for the period 1980-81/1988-89 has been related to the Block Account of the zonal railways in 1980-81 and the following ratios calculated -

a) Ratio of the Block Account of a zonal railway to the total Block Account of Indian Railways. For example, ratio of CR Block Account to Block Account of IR as a whole in 1980-81 was 14.05.

b) Ratio of DRF expenditure of a zonal railway to the Total DRF expenditure of Indian Railways. For example, ratio of DRF expenditure on CR between 1980-81 and 1992-93 to DRF expenditure on IR for the same period was 14.99.

c) Ratio of DRF expenditure of zonal railway to its Block Account in 1980-81. For example,the ratio of DRF expenditure on CR between 1980-81 and 1992-93 to its Block Account in 1980-81 was 227.14.

Table 36

DRF and Block Account 1980-81 to 92-93

Rly.	*Block Account 1980-81*		*DRF 80-81/1992-93*		
	Amount	*% to IR*	*Amount*	*% to IR*	*% to Blk.Act.*
CR	1010.26	14.05	2294.74	14.99	227.14
ER	814.14	11.32	2214.36	14.46	271.99
NR	1000.71	13.92	2223.94	14.52	222.24
NE	360.44	5.01	826.34	5.40	229.26
NF	352.34	4.90	674.58	4.41	191.46
SR	728.10	10.13	1498.02	9.78	205.74
SC	690.57	9.60	1357.96	8.87	196.64
SE	1256.13	17.48	2320.24	15.15	184.71
WR	977.36	13.59	1902.95	12.42	194.70
IR	7190.03	100.00	15313.13	100.00	212.98

A railway having higher ratio of DRF expenditure to its Block Account would obviously have a better condition profile of assets than a railway having lower ratio of DRF expenditure to its Block Account.

The following points are observed from Table 6 above.

a) Ratio of DRF expenditure of zonal railways to Total DRF expenditure of Indian Railways was more or less in the same ratio as its ratio of Block Account to Total Block Account of Indian Railways except in two or possibly three cases viz. ER and SE.

b) Ratio of DRF expenditure on a zonal railway to its Block Account was the highest on ER and lowest on SE railway. There were four railways which had ratios higher than IR Average, and others had lower than IR Average.

This means that at the end of the period assets on CR, ER, NR and WR were in a better condition than on such railways as SE. This could perhaps be justified if the density of traffic on these railways was higher than other railways such that the condition profile of the assets on these railways had been more adversely affected, or as a consequence of the heavier DRF expenditure the operating expenses showed better results.

Table 37 shows the ratio of DRF expenditure during the period to the Block Account at the beginning of the period and the Index of Operating Expenses (not the same as Operating Ratio) to the Operating Expenses in the Base Year. It needs to be clarified that only such operating expenses which may be affected by DRF expenditure have been taken for this purpose viz. Demand Nos. 4 to 12. Basic data are in Annexure-35 and Table 36. The railways have been arranged in ascending order.

Table 37

Ratio of DRF to Block Account		*Index of Operating Expenses*	
SE	184.71	NF	189.70
NF	191.46	SR	214.57
WR	194.70	SE	220.56
SC	196.64	SC	221.15
SR	205.75	ER	233.33
NR	222.24	NE	240.08
CR	227.14	NR	250.00
NE	229.26	WR	251.72
ER	271.99	CR	252.33
IR	212.98	IR	234.86

In the above Table -

a) Lowest Ratio of DRF to Block Account was on SE. But still the Index of Operating Expenses was the third lowest.

b) The Ratio of DRF to its Block Account was highest on ER. As a result thereof the Index of Operating Expenses on ER should have been the lowest. But this is not so. Which implies that full benefits of renewals and replacement expenses were not realised.

c) NF had the second lowest ratio of DRF to Block Account. This would normally imply that in 1992-93 its assets were not in as good condition as the other railways which had a higher ratio of DRF expenditure to Block Account. This should have resulted in a higher index of increase in operating expenses as compared to those railways. This has not happened. This may perhaps be because of higher induction of "capital" on NF than on many other railways. This is borne out by the position in the previous chapter. Same applies to SR also.

It is normally expected that a railway having higher ratio of DRF expenditure to its Block Account will have its assets in better condition and therefore lower index of increase of operating expenses and vice versa. But this is not borne out by the above results.

a) The three highest ratio of DRF to Block Account railways are CR, NE and ER while the three railways with lowest index of operating expenses are NF, SR and SE.

b) The three lowest ratio of DRF to Block Account are SE, NF and WR while the three railways with highest index of operating expenses are NR, WR and CR.

Let us now see the Ratio of DRF to the Block Account in relation to Density of Traffic. Relating DRF expenditure to Density of Traffic only may not, at first sight, appear reasonable. However, in view of the fact that on an average more than 80% of the DRF expenditure is on Permanent Way & Works, Motive Power and Carriage and Wagon, it would not be wrong to relate DRF expenditure to Density of Traffic - as an indicator of asset use. This is shown in Table 38. Base data are in Annexures-36 & Table 36.

Table 38

Ratio of DRF to Block Account		*Density of Traffic (Mil. TU/ETKM)*	
ER	271.99	NR	3.38
NE	229.26	CR	3.37
CR	227.14	WR	3.34
NR	222.24	SE	2.65
SR	205.75	SC	2.57
SC	196.64	NE	2.53
WR	194.70	ER	2.43
NF	191.46	SR	2.12
SE	184.71	NF	1.43
IR	212.98	IR	2.80

It may be seen from the above Table that

a) NF had the lowest density of traffic and second lowest ratio of DRF to Block Account.

b) SR had the second lowest density but its ratio of DRF to Block Account was higher than on NR, CR, NE and ER all of which had higher density of traffic.

c) NR had the highest density and its ratio of DRF was neither the highest nor the lowest.

d) CR had the second highest density of traffic and its ratio of DRF to Block Account was lower than on NE and ER.

e) ER had the highest ratio of DRF to Block Account but its density of traffic was the third lowest.

As discussed earlier, DRF expenditure should also be governed by asset condition profile of a railway, broadly indicated by density of traffic (presuming age profile of assets of all the railways to be more or less the same). This however is not borne out by the situation encountered above.

We can now rank the railways based on the different criteria. This is shown in Table 39.

Table 39

Ranking of Railway for DRF Expenditure 1992-93

Density of Tfc.	*Raito of*			*Index of Op. Expenses*
	Blk Act. to IR	*DRF to IR*	*DRF to Blk.Act.*	*88-89/92-93*
NR	SE	SE	ER	NF
CR	CR	CR	NE	SR
WR	NR	NR	CR	SE
SE	WR	ER	NR	SC
SC	ER	WR	SR	ER
NE	SR	SR	SC	NE
ER	SC	SC	WR	NR
SR	NE	NE	NF	WR
NF	NF	NF	SE	CR

The Railways have been arranged in order of most favourable to least favourable positon. Thus, first four columns in descending order and the last column in ascending order.

As would be seen from the above Table, no pattern seems to emerge except in case of the second and third columns. Is this because no pattern is legitimately possible or does it indicate the absence of a policy regarding DRF expenditure ?

SECTION 2 : PERIOD 1980-81 TO 1988-89

It would now be appropriate to examine the relationship between investment share and productivity of the zonal railways. The relationship according to all four methods has been traced below.

Annexure-22 shows whether the investment share of the zonal railway was HIGH, EQUAL or LOW. And the calculation of capital output ratios is in Annexure-24. Based on these, the following relationship has been found - Table 40.

Table 40

Total Investment and Productivity 80-81/88-89

Rly.	*ACOR*		*ICOR*		*INDCOR*		*INDICOR*	
	Inv. Share	*Prod.*	*Inv. Share*	*Prod.*	*Inv. Share*	*Prod.*	*Inv. Share*	*Prod.*
CR	L	H	L	E	L	E	L	L
ER	H	L	H	E	H	E	H	E
NR	L	H	L	H	L	E	L	E
NE	E	E	E	E	E	H	E	H
NF	H	L	H	L	H	E	H	H
SR	H	L	H	L	H	E	H	E
SC	E	E	E	E	E	E	E	E
SE	H	E	H	H	H	H	H	H
WR	L	H	L	E	L	E	L	L

The above relationships are more clearly shown in the following Charts.

Chart 17

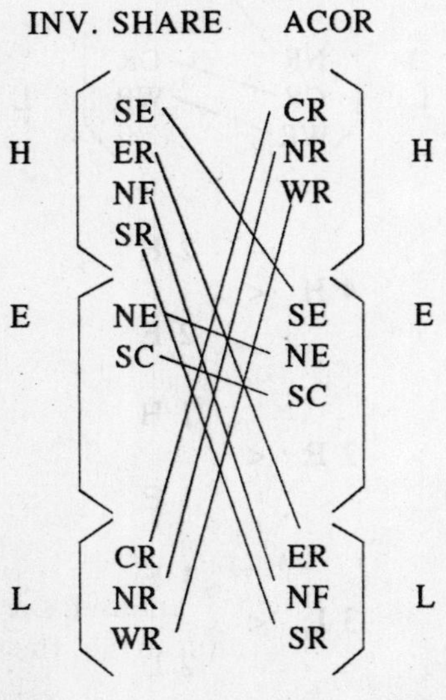

Chart 18

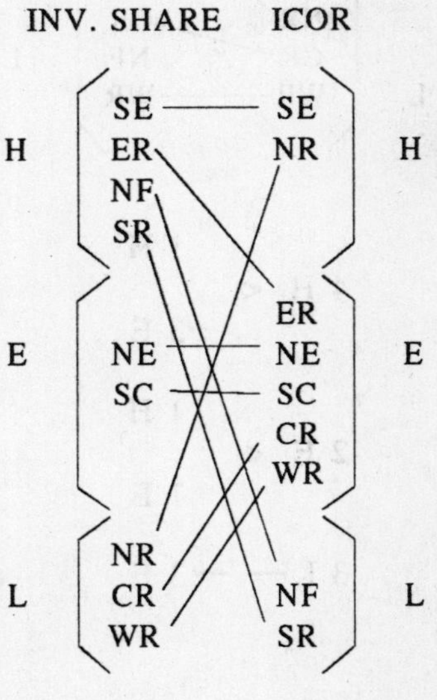

4 H < 1 E, 3 L

2 E —————— 2 E

3 L —————— 3 H

4 H < 1 H, —— 1 E, 2 L

2 E ———— 2 E

3 L < 1 H, 2 E

Chart 19

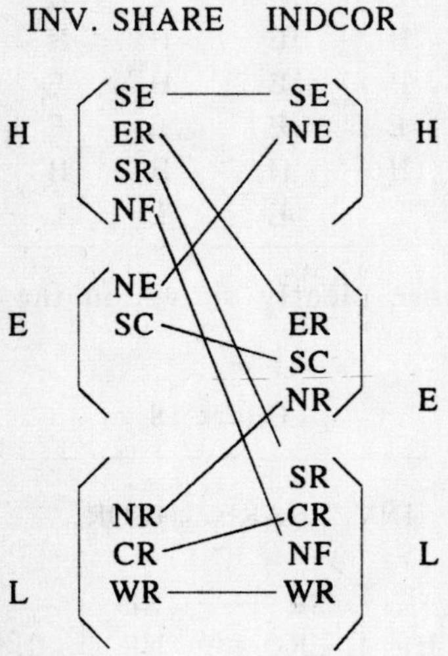

4 H < 1 H, 3 E

2 E < 1 H, 1 E

3 L —— —3 E

Chart 20

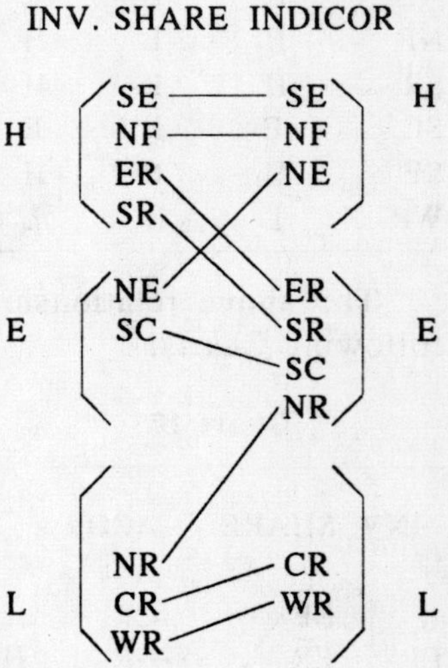

4 H < 2 H, 2 E

2 E < 1 H, 1 E

3 L < 1 E, 2 L

Productivity Matrices

Putting the above relationship in a Railway-wise Productivity Matrix we get the following results - Table 41.

Table 41

Railway-wise Productivity Matrix

	HH	*HE*	*HL*	*EH*	*EE*	*EL*	*LH*	*LE*	*LL*
CR							1	2	1
ER		3	1						
NR							2	2	
NE				2	2				
NF	1	1	2						
SR		2	2						
SC					4				
SE	3	1							
WR							1	2	1
	4	7	5	2	6	-	4	6	2

The following points may be noted

a) CR, NR and WR had LOW investment share. This may be contrasted with the investment share when Capital only was considered, where NR had EQUAL investment share and CR and WR had LOW investment share.

b) SC was always in HL catgegory for Capital, whereas it is in EE category when Total Investments are considered.

c) If capital only is considered, ER received EQUAL investment. If total investment is considered, ER received HIGH investment

The above matrix is further summarised in a Productivity Matrix irrespective of railways or method - Table 42.

Table 42

Productivity Matrix

		Productivity			
		H	E	L	
	H	4	7	5	16
Investment	E	2	6	-	8
Share	L	4	6	2	12
		10	19	7	

The following conclusions emerge from the above matrix -

a) HIGH investment share led to HIGH productivity in 25% cases and and HIGH plus EQUAL productivity in 70% cases and LOW productivity in 30% cases.

b) EQUAL investment share led to 100% HIGH plus EQUAL Productivity.

c) LOW investment share in 33% cases led to HIGH and in 85% cases HIGH plus EQUAL productivity.

d) For HIGH productivity HIGH or LOW investment share are most promising, but not EQUAL investment share. This conclusion, however, is not logical - because it implies that while it is good to have HIGH or LOW investment share, EQUAL investment share should be avoided. This is illogical and can only be explained as a statistical freak.

e) However, if HIGH and EQUAL productivities are taken together, EQUAL investment share gives the best results. It may be noticed that while HIGH and LOW investment gave some cases of LOW productivity, there was no case of LOW productivity when investment share was EQUAL.

f) Highest percentage of LOW productivity is obtained when investment share is HIGH.

SECTION 3 : PERIOD 1988-89/92-93

The method followed in Section 2 of Chapter-6 has been followed here also. That is, the Average Traffic Unit and Average Total Investment has been calculated for the period 1988-89/92-93 and adopted as base for evaluation of data for 1992-93.

Average Traffic Unit calculations are at Annexure-11 Average Total Investment calculations are at Annexure-13. The Investment Share calculations are at Annexure-23 and the Productivity of Average Total Investment calculations are at Annexure-25. The relationship between investment share and productivity under the four concepts of capital output ratio are shown below.

A. Average Capital Output Ratio (ACOR)

The following relationship has been found under ACOR.

Table 43

RLY.	*INV.SHARE*	*ACOR*
CR	L	H
ER	E	L
NR	E	E
NF	H	L
SR	H	L
SC	E	E
SE	E	E
WR	L	H

See Annexures-23 & 25

Chart 21

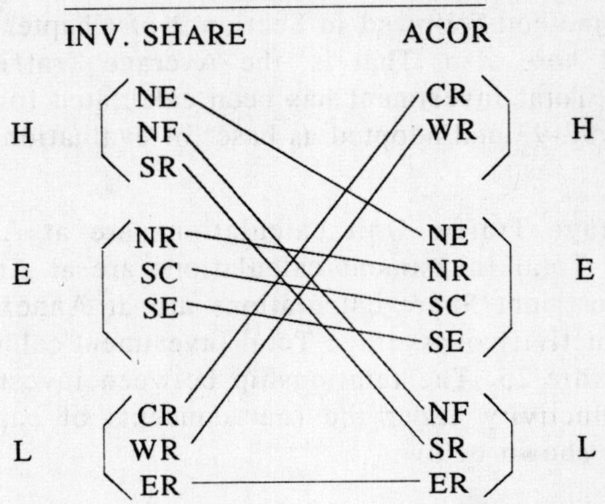

The relationship obtained in Table 43 has been shown in Chart 21. This is summarised as under

H3 < E1 / L2	E4 < E3 / L1	L2 — — H2

B. Incremental Capital Output Ratio (ICOR)

The following relationship has been found under ICOR.

Table 44

RLY.	*INV.SHARE*	*ICOR*
CR	L	H
ER	E	E
NR	E	L
NE	H	L
NF	H	L
SR	H	L
SC	E	H
SE	E	H
WR	L	L

See Annexures-23 & 25

Chart 22

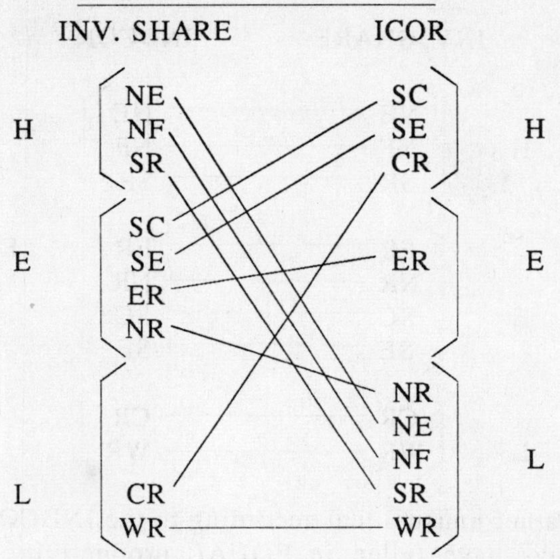

The relationship obtained in Table 44 has been shown in Chart 22 and summarised as under

H 3—— —L 3   E 4 <—— E 1 (H 2, L 1)   L 2 < (H 1, L 1)

C. Indexed Capital Output Ratio (INDCOR)

The following relationship has been found under INDCOR.

Table 45

RLY.	*INV.SHARE*	*INDCOR*
CR	L	E
ER	E	E
NR	E	E
NE	H	E
NF	H	E
SR	H	E
SC	E	E
SE	E	E
WR	L	E

See Annexures-23 & 25

Chart 23

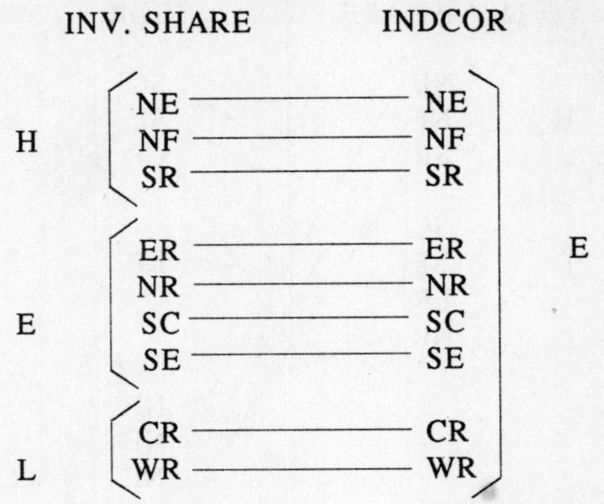

It is rather unusual that according to the INDCOR method all railways have fallen in EQUAL productivity category. However, the summarised position of investment share and productivity is as under

H 3 — — E 3 E 4 — — E 4 L 2 — — E 2

D. Incremental Capital Output Ratio (INDICOR)

The following relationship has been found under INDICOR.

Table 46

RLY.	*INV.SHARE*	*INDICOR*
CR	L	H
ER	E	H
NR	E	L
NE	H	L
NF	H	E
SR	H	L
SC	E	H
SE	E	H
WR	L	L

See Annexures-23 & 25

Chart 24

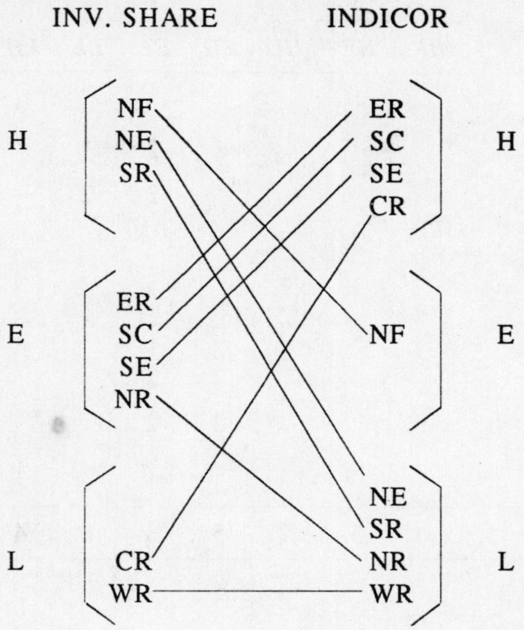

The relationship found in Chart 24 can be summarised as under :

	E 1		H 3		H 1
H 3 <		E 4 <		L 2<	
	L 2		L 1		L 1

Productivity Matrices

The relationships obtained under all the four methods have been combined to get two matrices - a Railway-wise Productivity Matrix irrespective of the method of calculating productivity and second a Productivity Matrix irrespective of railway and method.

Table 47

Railway-wise Productivity Matrix

RLY.	*HH*	*HE*	*HL*	*EH*	*EE*	*EL*	*LH*	*LE*	*LL*
CR							3	1	
ER				1	2	1			
NR					2	2			
NE		2	2						
NF		2	2						
SR		1	3						
SC				2	2				
SE				2	2				
WR							1	1	2
Total		5	7	5	8	3	4	2	2

The results are quite distributed. The only observations of significance are that

a) CR received LOW investment share but its productivity was HIGH 75% of the times.

b) Only NE, NF and SR received HIGH investment share. None of them got HIGH productivity also. While NE and NF had EQUAL and LOW productivity equally distributed, in case of SR productivity was LOW in 75% cases.

c) CR and WR received LOW investment share. CR has been discussed earlier. In case of WR the results of productivity were more or less evenly distributed between HIGH, EQUAL and LOW.

Summarising the results for all railways and all methods we get the following Productivity Matrix.

Table 48

Productivity Matrix

		Productivity			
		H	E	L	
	H	-	5	7	12
Investment	E	5	8	3	16
Share	L	4	2	2	8
		9	15	12	

The following points may be noted. Looking at it from the point of Investment share

a) In no case HIGH investment share led to HIGH productivity. In 58% cases it led to LOW productivity and in 42% cases EQUAL productivity

b) EQUAL investment share led to HIGH productivity in 31% cases, EQUAL productivity in 50% cases and LOW productivity in 19% cases .

c) LOW investment share led to HIGH productivity in 50% cases and EQUAL and LOW productivity in 25% cases each.

Looking at it from the point of Productivity

d) For HIGH productivity, investment share must never be HIGH.

e) For EQUAL productivity EQUAL investment share is desirable.

f) LOW productivity will accrue if investment share is HIGH.

8

Conclusions

IN Chapter-6 the productivity of Capital-at-charge was evaluated for two time periods 1970-71 to 88-89 and then 1988-89 to 92-93. In Chapter-7 the productivity of Total Investment was also evaluated for two periods 1980-81 to 88-89 and then 1988-89 to 1992-93. In both cases, slightly different methodology was adopted for the period 1988-89 to 1992-93. In each case the analysis was conducted for four concepts of productivity. Certain trends were found and some conclusions were drawn.

In this Chapter the results of the two time periods have been combined. It is realised that this kind of combining of results of different methods, different time periods, different investments is not very correct. It is more of statistical than economic nature. But it is still being done because what has been fundamentally attempted in the last two chapters is to examine the validity of a hypothesis made in Chapter-5 that investments on a railway as a ratio of total investments on IR should not be higher than the ratio of its traffic units to total traffic units of IR over a period of time, otherwise the effect on capital productivity would be adverse. It is this hypothesis which is central to the study and not the method or the time period etc. Therefore, many time slices and many concepts and methodologies have been taken and their results combined so that peculiarities of individual time slices, concepts and methods get, at least theoretically, neutralised. The results obtained and conclusions drawn can then be legitimately said to be more generalised and reliable.

CAPITAL-AT-CHARGE

Here the Productivity matrices in Section 1 and Section 2 of Chapter-6 have been combined to get Railway-wise Productivity Matrix for Capital-at-Charge which is given below.

Table 49
Railway-wise Productivity Matrix

RLY.	*HH*	*HE*	*HL*	*EH*	*EE*	*EL*	*LH*	*LE*	*LL*	*Score*
CR				8			4	3	1	83
ER				1	3		3	7	2	86
NR	3	1		6	1	1	4			76
NE				1	7	8				57
NF		4	8		1	3				41
SR		2	14							34
SC		2	14							34
SE	3		1	4	3	5				61
WR				3	1		4	4	4	79
Total	6	9	37	23	16	17	15	14	7	551

Scoring System

Each railway has different pattern of investment share and productivity combination represented by letters HL, EH etc. A straight comparisons of the patterns is difficult. For example, how can one say whether the CR pattern above should be considered better than NR pattern. It is not possible to make such a straight comparison. However, we may do so by adopting a scoring system by putting values on investment shares and productivities.

Investment Share Value

Since LOW investment share is preferable to EQUAL investment share which in turn is preferable to HIGH investment share, we may adopt the following values for investment share.

HIGH	1
EQUAL	2
LOW	3

Productivity Value

Since HIGH productivity is preferable to EQUAL productivity which is preferable to LOW productivity we may adopt the following values for productivity.

HIGH	3
EQUAL	2
LOW	1

Thus, a HE investment share - productivity combination will have the following value.

$$HE = 1 + 2 = 3$$

Needless to say a higher combination value is preferable to lower combination value. The full range of investment share productivity combination values will be

HH	4
HE	3
HL	2
EH	5
EE	4
EL	3
LH	6
LE	5
LL	4

It may be noticed that the following groups of combinations have the values indicated against each —

Group	Value
LH	6
LE, EH	5
LL, HH, EE	4
HE, EL	3
HL	2

One feature of the groups and their values need to be noted. They indicate that 'upward looking situations' i.e. lower level investment share EQUAL or LOW leading to higher level productivity HIGH or EQUAL respectively -are preferable to 'downward looking situations' i.e. HIGH or EQUAL investment share leading to EQUAL or LOW productivity respectively. There is not much to choose between same level situations i.e. HIGH - HIGH, EQUAL - EQUAL or LOW - LOW, hence they have average kind of value i.e.4.

The above may also be represented through the following matrix.

Table 50

Productivity

		H	E	L
	H	4	3	2
Investment	E	5	4	3
Share	L	6	5	4

Based on the above system of values the score of each railway is given in the last column of Table 49. The railways may then be arranged in descending order of score are as follows.

Table 51

Railway	Score		
ER	86		
CR	83		
WR	79	Maximum	96
NR	76	Average	64
SE	61	Minimum	32
NE	57		
NF	41		
SR	34		
SC	34		
IR Avg.	61		

There are a total of 16 occurrences of investment share - productivity combination for each railway. If an average situation combination i.e. EE is taken, the average score works out to 64. Maximum score possible is 96 and minimum is 32. The relative performance of the railways, the extent of difference between the highest and the lowest score and the deviations from average performance need to be noted in the above tabulation.

The Railway-wise Productivity Matrix of Table 49 is summarised to get Productivity Matrix irrespective of railway and methods of computation in Table 52 below.

Table 52

Productivity Matrix

		Productivity			
		H	E	L	
Investment Share	H	6	9	37	52
	E	23	16	17	56
	L	15	14	7	36
		44	39	61	

The following conclusions may be drawn from the above matrix.

From the point of investment share -

* If investment share is HIGH there are overwhelming chances that productivity will be LOW

* If investment share is EQUAL there are better chances of productivity being HIGH, than being EQUAL or LOW

* If investment share is LOW there are better chances of productivity being HIGH or EQUAL and about 20% chances of it being LOW.

From the point of productivity

* For HIGH productivity investment share should decidedly not be HIGH.

* LOW productivity will result if investment share is HIGH

Thus, it may be seen that HIGH investment share must definitely be avoided.

TOTAL INVESTMENT

Continuing the analysis on the same pattern as above for Total Investment also, we get the following matrix by combining the results for period 1980-81 to 88-89 and 88-89 to 92-93 obtained in Section 2 and Section 3 of Chapter-7.

Table 53

Railway-wise Productivity Matrix

RLY.	*HH*	*HE*	*HL*	*EH*	*EE*	*EL*	*LH*	*LE*	*LL*	*Score*
CR							4	3	1	43
ER		3	1	1	2	1				31
NR					2	2	2	2		36
NE		2	2	2	2					28
NF	1	3	4							21
SR		3	5							19
SC				2	6					30
SE	3	1		2	2					33
WR						2	3	3		39
Total	4	12	12	7	14	3	8	8	4	280

The score in the last column has been computed on the basis of the same value system as adopted in the previous section. Arranging the railways in descending order of score we get the following

Table 54

Railway	Score
CR	43
WR	39
NR	36
SE	33
ER	31
SC	30
NE	28
NF	21
SR	19
IR Avg.	31

Maximum 48
Average 32
Minimum 16

There are eight occurrences of investment share - productivity combination for each railway. The average score of a railway would thus be 32. Maximum score possible is 48 and the minimum is 16. In the light of this, the performance of each railway may be evaluated. The results are self evident and no further comments are necessary.

The results of Table 53 above are summarised in the following Productivity Matrix irrespective of railway and method of computation.

Table 55

Productivity Matrix

		Productivity H	Productivity E	Productivity L	
Investment Share	H	4	12	12	28
	E	7	14	3	24
	L	8	8	4	20
		19	34	19	

The following points in the above matrix need to be noted.

From the point of investment share :

* If investment share is HIGH, the chances of productivity also being HIGH are very little.
* If investment share is EQUAL, there are very strong chances that productivity will also be EQUAL. There are very little chances of it being LOW.
* If investment share is LOW, the chances of productivity also being LOW are very small.

From the point of productivity

* For HIGH productivity investment share should be with LOW or EQUAL but not HIGH.
* For EQUAL productivity, investment share should also preferably be EQUAL.
* LOW productivity will result if investment share is HIGH.

General

Data regarding traffic unit and investment have been analysed for many different periods and in many different ways. Two kinds of unmistakable conclusions can be drawn - one dealing with general trends and the other dealing with performance of individual railways. Both have policy implications.

As regards the general trend two phenomena have been clearly established that -

a) There is a definite relationship between investment share, traffic unit share and productivity of a railway.

b) The relationship is such that if ratio of investment on a railway to total investment on IR is higher than the ratio of its traffic unit to total traffic of IR then there will be adverse effect on the productivity of that railway.

Thus, the hypothesis made at the beginning of the study stands validated.

As regards performance of individual railways, the investment share - productivity scores shown in Table 51 and Table 54 are self explanatory. We may concentrate on Table 54 only, which deals with Total Investment, as investments from 'capital' are now fast dwindling and may soon become negligible or vanish altogether. It shows that

a) Productivity on SE, ER and SC are more or less of average category.

b) Productivity on NF and SR are decidedly poor.

c) It is surprising that SR has turned out to be much less capital productive than even NE and NF which are traditionally regarded as one of the least productive railways. Actually, this result has been observed throughout the study irrespective of period or method or whether the analysis is for capital-at-charge or for Total investment.

While policy implications of the general trend are in setting up a macro criteria for resource allocation the implication arising out of performance of individual railways appears to be that not only the investment proposals of SR & NF need to be more carefully evaluated, perhaps a separate set of policy guide lines may be necessary for these railways.

9

Resource Allocation

THE resource allocation process on Indian Railways has been briefly described in Chapter-2. As will be seen, it has all the ingredients of an ideal system. There is a Corporate Plan and Five Year Plans. There is a top-to-bottom approach characterised by policy circulars, annual fund indication etc. The Zonal railways are expected to frame their investment proposals keeping the fund indication in view. There is also a bottom-to-top approach. Each investment proposal is framed and financially evaluated at the lowest rung of the ladder i.e. the Division and discussed at zonal level as well as at the level of Ministry of Railways and in major cases with the Planning Commission.

But still as shown earlier, overcapitalisation and undercapitalisation on railways have resulted as reflected by the capital output ratios. It has been contended in Chapter-5 that this has been basically because of almost total focus on micro and total shadowing of macro aspects of investment.

One purpose of the study was to find whether any macro criteria could be developed which may be used for determining allocation of resources amongst the zonal railways. In the study it has been found that there is a relationship between the traffic share of a railway, its investment share and its capital productivity such that investments on a railway should not be

HIGHER than its share of traffic. It needs to be examined whether the above relationship can be used for resource allocation purposes.

Actually, rejection of HIGH investment share option leaves us with two other options viz. EQUAL and LOW investment shares. However, having LOW investment share on all the railways is statistically impossible and if there are some LOW investment share railways, there are bound to be some HIGH investment share railways also. And since HIGH investment share situation has already been rejected. Logically LOW investment share option also must be simultaneously rejected.

This leaves us with only one option i.e. EQUAL investment share. The investment share and traffic share proposition can then be restated to say that - the investment share of a railway should more or less be EQUAL to its traffic share.

Let us apply the above criteria to 1995-96 Budget Estimates as approved by Parliament and see what would have been the allocation if it had been done on the basis of this criteria.

Table 56

Total Gross Investment Budget Estimate 1995-96

(Rs.Lakhs)

Rly.	*As approved*		*On criteria*		*Diff.*
	Amount	*% to total*	*Av. TU Ratio*	*Amount*	
	1	2	3	4	5
CR	110270	13.21	17.61	146948	(+) 36678
ER	100844	12.08	10.41	86867	(-) 13967
NR	127611	15.29	17.14	143026	(+) 15415
NE	39555	4.74	4.71	39303	(-) 252
NF	43700	5.24	2.56	21362	(-) 22338
SR	80975	9.70	6.62	55241	(-) 25734
SC	98853	11.85	10.01	83529	(-) 15324
SE	124897	14.97	15.49	129259	(+) 4362
WR	107755	12.92	15.45	128925	(+) 21170
Total	834460			834460	

Budget Estimates for the year 1994-95 is at Annexure-37. The column 'Av. TU Ratio' in Table 56 above is the ratio of Average TU of a railway for the period 1988-89/1992-93 to the Average TU of IR for the same period. Details are in Annexure-11. As per the proposed criteria, investments on the railways should be in this ratio. The amount of investment so computed is shown in column 4 of the above Table. The difference in ratios and the amounts may be seen.

Acceptance of the criteria would imply that investments on some railways should be scaled down and on some railways stepped up.

It is possible to argue that scaling down investment will retard the growth of traffic. This apprehension does not stand closer scrutiny. It needs to be remembered that for most of the traffic that the railways carry viz. bulk goods, long distance passengers etc., the demand is rather inelastic. There are reasonably good chances that much of additional traffic of this kind will come to railways. If this happens and the infrastructure does not grow due to curtailed investment, conditions of 'congestion' will arise. Upto a point a railway systemn is usually flexible enough to tolerate 'congestion' without significant effect on performance level. By the time conditions of 'congestion' arise, simultaneously ipso facto traffic unit share of the railway would also go up (unless similar 'congestion' is experienced by other railways due to overall curtailment of investment, which of course is an entirely different scenario). This will, according to the proposed criteria, automatically justify increased investment on that railway, thereby relieving congestion. In fact the proposed criteria has the potentiality of leading to an equilibrium situation in the long run. There might be a time lag between appearance of 'congestion' and its relief. But this is more a problem of timely recognition of symptoms and initiation of corrective action than the criteria itself.

As a corrolary to the scaling down of investment argument discussed above, it is also possible to say that the proposition that investment share should be raised to correspond with traffic share where the former is lower than the latter is not by itself acceptable because investments should be made only if the traffic potential so warrants. Therefore, if traffic potential does not warrant, there is no reason to increase investment even if investment share is less than traffic share. In response it can only be said that there is no argument with the fact that traffic potential is of fundamental importance. Actually the proposition made does not at all contravene this consideration. On the contrary, it reinforces it. Because, it is more likely that a railway having a higher traffic share has a higher traffic potential also than a railway having lower traffic share. For example, SE railway definitely has a higher traffic potential than NF railway. Therefore, it is certainly possible to say that broadly speaking a unit of investment on SE is more likely to generate more traffic than on NF railway. Beyond this, the actual position will depend upon the Laws of Diminishing Return and Marginal Productivity of capital operating on those railways at that time.

Adopting the proposed criteria has an additional advantage. It would be possible to delegate more decision making powers to where they rightfully belong i.e. the zonal railways. Once it is accepted that investments on a railway should be more or less in the ratio of its traffic share, it is only the total amount of investments in different railways which need be approved by the Railway Board. Approval of individual investment proposals, as at present may be dispensed with. It may be left with the zonal railways. In certain cases, however, approval of individual investment proposal by the Board may still be desirable e.g. major projects, projects involving more than one railway, technology upgradation projects etc. Determining the type of cases where decision at the level of Railway Board may be necessary is a matter of detail. But a significant shift towards greater decentralisation will become possible without sacrificing productivity considerations. In fact, productivity consideration will acquire greater importance than hitherto. Higher the productivity of a railway larger the investible funds that it may expect.

In view of the foregoing, it is felt that the conclusions of this study are quite valid and the proposition, that investment share of a railway should more or less be equal to its traffic share, should be adopted for allocation of investible resources amongst the zonal railways. Some clarifications, however, are necessary.

a) The criteria may not be always applicable. Deviations may have to be made in the short run. In fact its strict application may sometimes lead to avoidable delay in execution of some projects and may thus turn out to be actually counter-productive. But over a longer period of time investment shares should correspond to traffic shares. The criteria may most fruitfully be applied to, say, the Five Year Plans and through it to the Annual Plans.

b) The criteria suggested is in no way an alternative to the existing system. It supplements the existing system in determining the total plan size of a railway. In a way it, so to say, acts as an envelope to the existing system. The sum total of individual investment proposals - both new as well as on going - should remain within this overall total limit or the 'envelope'.

c) It does not help to decide the size of the cake but only its distribution. It does not help to decide what should be the Plan size of Indian Railways as a whole. But having decided the Plan size, it offers a broad guideline in allocating the resources to the zonal railways and thereby detrermine their Plan size. Once their Plan size is determined, the zonal railways may be required to structure their investments - the Plan Heads - in such a manner as to keep within the Plan size and still produce the output. It is definitely possible to structure the investment plans on these lines.

There is no better way of concluding this study than to once again recall the observations of the Committee on Capital Output Ratio.

"The COR / ICOR trends for the railways, if analysed properly at micro and macro levels would go a long way in providing Railway Management suitable guidance for *inter zonal and inter-departmental resource allocation* and at the same time would also help in the perspective planning and economic modelling" (emphasis mine)

Actually this should become a part of the top down process itself and may gainfully be extended even to the Divisions after suitable data base is built up.

Annexures

Annexure - 1

GLOSSARY OF TERMS

Capital-at-charge	Non-refundable loan from Government of India for creation of assets.
Capital Ratio	Ratio of incremental capital-at-charge on a railway to total incremental capital-at-charge of Indian Railways during the period under consideration.
Capital Index	Index of capital-at-charge of a railway at the end of the period with respect to its own capital-at-charge at the beginning of the period.
NTKM	Net Tonne Kilometers represents movement of one tonne of freight for one kilometer.
PKM	Passenger Kilometer represents movement of one passenger for one kilometer.
Traffic Units (TU)	Converted Units in the following ratio 1 Net Tonne KM Freight = 1 TU 1 Non Suburban Passenger KM = 0.50 TU 1 Suburban Passenger KM = 0.25 TU
TU Ratio	Ratio of a railway's TU to total TU of Indian Railways
TU Index	Index of TU at the end of the period on a railway with respect to its own TU at the beginning of the period
Operating Expenses	Unlike Operating Ratio of Indian Railway statistics, Operating Expenses include only such elements of repairs, maintenance and running expenses which

	affect depreciation of assets viz. Demand Nos.4 to 12 of Heads of Demand.
Index of Operating Expenses	Index of Operating Expenses in the current year with respect to Operating Expenses in the base year.
Dividend	Annual payment by Indian Railways to GOI for loan capital received. It is in the nature of interest rather than dividend of commercial parlance.
Total Investment	Sum total of all investments financed out of loan or internal resources.
Loan Account	Accounting record showing only assets created act of loans from GOI to Railways.
Block Account	Accounting record showing assets created out of Capital, Development Fund, Accident Compensation Safety and Passenger Amenities Fund and Revenue as well as the 'improvement' element of the cost of assets financed out of Depreciation Reserve Fund.

ABBREVIATIONS

Funds

DRF	Depreciation Reserve Fund
DF	Development Fund
ACSPF	Accident Compensation Safety and Passenger Amenities Fund
OLWR	Open Line Works Revenue

Railway Zones

CR	Central Railway
ER	Eastern Railway
NR	Northern Railway
NE	North Eastern Railway
NF	North-East Frontier Railway
SR	Southern Railway
SC	South Central Railway
SE	South Eastern Railway
WR	Western Railway
IR	Indian Railways
GOI	Government of India
IRFC	Indian Railway Finance Corporation
CONCOR	Container Corporation of India

Annexure - 2

HEADS OF DEMANDS FOR GRANTS

Demand No.	*Description*
1	Railway Board
2	Research, Audit and Miscellaneous Establishment.
3	General Superintendence and Services on Railways.
4	Repairs & Maintenance of Way and Works.
5	Repairs & Maintenance of Motive Power
6	Repairs & Maintenance of Carriage & Wagon.
7	Repairs & Maintenance of Plant & Equipment.
8	Operating Exp. - Rolling Stock & Equipment.
9	Operating Exp. - Traffic
10	Operating Exp. - Fuel
11	Staff Welfare & Amenities
12	Miscellaneous Working Expenses
13	Provident Fund, Pension and other Retirement Benefits.
14	Appropriation to Funds.
15	Dividend to General Revenues.
16	Assets - Acquisition, Construction and Replacement.

Annexure - 3

PLAN HEADS AND SOURCES OF FINANCE

No.	*Plan Heads*	*Capital*	*DRF*	*DF*	*ACSPF*	*OLWR*
11	New Lines (Cons)	*	*		*	*
12	Purchase of new Lines					
13	Restoration of dismantled lines	*	*			
14	Gauge Conversion	*	*	*	*	*
15	Doubling	*	*	*	*	*
16	Traffic Facilities Yard Remodelling & Others	*	*	*	*	*
17	Computerisation	*		*		*
18	Railway Research	*	*	*		*
21	Rolling Stock	*	*	*		*
31	Track Renewals		*			*
32	Bridge Works	*	*	*	*	*
33	Signal & Telecom Works	*	*	*	*	*
34	Taking over line wires from P&T					
35	Electrification Projects	*	*	*	*	*
36	Other Elec. works	*	*	*	*	*
41	Machinery & Plant	*	*	*		*
42	W/shops incl. Prod.Units	*	*	*	*	*
51	Staff Quarters	*	*			*
52	Amenities for Staff	*	*	*		*
53	i) Passenger Amenities	*	*	*	*	
	ii) Other Rly.Users Amenities					
62	Inv.in Govt.Comm.Undertakings	*				
64	Other specified works	*	*	*	*	*
81	Metropolitan Transport Projects	*	*	*	*	*
71	Stores Suspense	*				
72	Manufacture Suspense	*				
73	Misc. Advance (capital)	*				

DRF & ACSPF for New Lines have been indicated by Southern Railway only in Works, Machinery and Rolling Stock Programmes Pt.II, 92-93.

ACSPF has been discontinued with effect from 1.4.93. Capital Fund has been created with effect from 1.4.93 to finance all Plan Heads which are now being financed through loan i.e. Capital.

Annexure - 4

TRAFFIC UNIT CALCULATIONS : 1970-71

Rev. Earning NTKM (M)				*PKM (M)*						*Grand*
	Gauge-wise		*Total*		*BG*	*MG*	*NG*	*Total*	*TU*	*Total TU*
	BG	16,252		S	8,252	-	-	8,252	2063	
CR	MG	238	16,523	NS	11,901	111	150	12,162	6081	24,667
	NG	33								
	BG	13,921		S	5,693	-	-	5,693	1423	
ER	NG	1	13,922	NS	9,732	-	54	9,786	4893	20,238
	BG	15,289		S	-	-	-	-		
NR	MG	1,282	16,591	NS	17,161	2,783	72	20,016	10,008	26,599
	NG	20								
NE	MG	3,564	3,564	NS	53	9,946	-	9,999	5,000	8,564
	BG	860		S	-	-	-			
NF	MG	2,335	3,195	NS	307	3,279	4	3,590	1,795	4,990
	BG	5,240		S	356	1,066	-	1,422	356	
SR	MG	2,844	8,084	NS	3,896	5,079	20	8,995	4,498	12,938
	BG	7,687		S	-	68	-	68	17	
SC	MG	2,191	9,908	NS	5,374	3,019	213	8,606	4,303	14,228
	NG	30								
	BG	22,760		S	746	-	-	746	187	
SE	NG	157	22,917	NS	6,244	-	440	6,684	3,342	26,446
	BG	9,541		S	6,871	-		6,871	1,718	
WR	MG	6,420	15,989	NS	8,100	6,732	398	15,230	7,615	25,322
	NG	28								
IR	All Gauges		110,693						53,299	163,992

Annexure - 5

TRAFFIC UNIT CALCULATIONS : 1980-81

Rev.	Earning NTKM (M) Gauge-wise		Total		PKM (M) BG	MG	NG	Total	TU	Grand Total TU
	BG	26,058		S	13,867	-	-	13,867	3467	
CR	MG	283	26,377	NS	27,856	202	411	28,469	14235	44,079
	NG	36								
	BG	14,663		S	9,234	-	-	9,234	2309	
ER	MG	-	14,664	NS	15,638	-	35	15,673	7837	24,810
	BG	22,831		S	-	-	-	-		
NR	MG	1,561	23,401	NS	31,428	4,416	70	35,914	17,957	41,358
	NG	9								
	BG	84		S	-		-			
NE	MG	3,685	3,769	NS	930	12,845		13,775	6,888	10,657
	BG	1,098		S	-	-	-			
NF	MG	2,008	3,106	NS	278	4,435	2	4,715	2,358	5,464
	BG	5,363		S	640	2,190	-	2,830	708	
SR	MG	2,323	7,686	NS	8,648	6,637	13	15,298	7,649	16,043
	BG	12,300		S	-		-	-	-	
SC	MG	2,251	14,551	NS	12,872	4,172	-	17,044	8,522	23,073
	BG	28,726		S	1,629	-	-	1,629	408	
SE	NG	86	24,812	NS	10,068	-	507	10,575	5,288	30,508
	BG	17,389		S	13,525	-	-	13,525	3,381	
WR	MG	6,855	24,288	NS	17,269	8,363	378	26,010	13,005	40,674
	NG	44								
IR	All Gauges		142,654						94,012	2,36,666

Annexure - 6

TRAFFIC UNIT CALCULATIONS : 1988-89

Rev.	*Earning NTKM (M) Gauge-wise*		*Total*		*PKM (M) BG*	*MG*	*NG*	*Total*	*TU*	*Grand Total TU*
	BG	36,691		S	17,238	-	-	17,238	4310	
CR	MG	17	36,708	NS	36,729	-	459	37,188	18594	59,612
	BG	25,678		S	11,618	-	-	11,681	2920	
ER	NG	-	25,678	NS	17,597	-	23	17,620	8810	37,408
	BG	35,521		S	35	-	-	35	9	
NR	MG	2,046	37,574	NS	37,529	6,425	123	44,077	22,039	59,622
	NG	7								
	BG	2,324		S	-	-	-			
NE	MG	3,463	5,787	NS	7,357	12,907	-	20,264	10,132	15,919
	BG	2,814		S	-	-	-			
NF	MG	3,102	5,916	NS	1,360	3,837	1	5,198	2,599	8,515
	BG	9,612		S	1,093	1,825	-	2,918	730	
SR	MG	2,290	11,902	NS	13,895	5,274	10	19,179	9,590	22,222
	BG	20,319		S	-	-	-	-	-	
SC	MG	2,489	22,808	NS	16,582	5,080	-	21,662	10,831	33,639
	BG	43,984		S	1,560	-	-	1,560	390	
SE	NG	112	44,096	NS	13,126	-	377	13,503	6,752	51,238
	BG	25,140		S	18,480	-	-	18,480	4,620	
WR	MG	6,761	31,904	NS	24,762	8,252	115	33,129	16,565	53,089
	NG	3								
IR	All Gauges		2,22,373						1,18,891	3,41,264

Annexure - 7

TRAFFIC UNIT CALCULATIONS : 1989-90

Rev.	*Earning NTKM (M)*	*Gauge-wise*	*Total*		*PKM (M)* *BG*	*MG*	*NG*	*Total*	*TU*	*Grand Total TU*
	BG	38,065		S	17,970	-	-	17,970	4,493	
CR	MG	-		NS	39,273	-	518	39,791	19,896	62,490
	NG	36	38,101							
	BG	25,441		S	12,534	-	-	12,534	3,134	
ER	MG	-		NS	18,203	-	22	18,225	9,113	37,688
	NG	-	25,441							
	BG	35,504		S	36	-	-	36	9	
NR	MG	2,410		NS	41,422	6,672	123	48,217	24,109	62,037
	NG	5	37,919							
	BG	2,686		S	-	-	-	-	-	
NE	MG	3,672		NS	8,083	13,049	-	21,132	10,566	16,924
	NG	-	6,358							
	BG	3,020		S	-	-	-	-	-	
NF	MG	3,216		NS	1,556	4,054	2	5,612	2,806	9,042
	NG	-	6,236							
	BG	9,867		S	1,251	1,995	-	3,246	812	
SR	MG	2,131	11998	NS	14,756	5,626	9	20,391	10,196	23,009
	BG	20,901		S	-	-	-	-	-	
SC	MG	2,435		NS	17,942	5,115	-	23,057	11,529	34,865
	NG	-	23,336							
	BG	47,349		S	1,702	-	-	-	426	
SE	MG	-		NS	13,953	-	414	14,367	7,184	55,067
	NG	108	47,457							
	BG	25,299		S	19,315	-	-	19,315	4,829	
WR	MG	7,454		NS	25,514	9,619	120	35,253	17,627	55,209
	NG	-	32,753							
IR	All Gauges									356,331

Annexure - 8

TRAFFIC UNIT CALCULATIONS : 1990-91

Rev.	*Earning NTKM (M)*				*PKM (M)*					*Grand*
		Gauge-wise	*Total*		*BG*	*MG*	*NG*	*Total*	*TU*	*Total TU*
	BG	39,925		S	18,971	-	-	18,971	4,743	
CR	MG	-		NS	42,858	-	587	43,445	21,723	66,424
	NG	33	39,958							
	BG	24,652		S	13,892	-	-	13,892	3,473	
ER	MG	-		NS	18,514	-	22	18,536	9,268	37,393
	NG	-	24,652							
	BG	36,183		S	39	-	-	39	10	
NR	MG	2,682		NS	41,980	6,497	128	48,605	24,303	63,182
	NG	4	38,869							
	BG	2,822		S	-	-	-	-	-	
NE	MG	3,910		NS	8,213	13,085	-	21,298	10,649	17,381
	NG	-	6,732							
	BG	2,991		S	-	-	-	-	-	
NF	MG	3,246		NS	2,062	3,533	2	5,597	2,799	9,036
	NG	-	6,237							
	BG	10,979		S	1,332	2,061	-	3,393	1,697	
SR	MG	2,220		NS	15,649	5,989	12	21,650	10,825	25,721
	NG	-	13,199							
	BG	22,037		S	-	-	-	-	-	
SC	MG	2,308		NS	20,170	5,491	-	25,661	12,831	37,176]
	NG	-	24,345							
	BG	48,578		S	1,792	-	-	1,792	448	
SE	MG	-		NS	14,602	-	402	15,004	7,502	56,623
	NG	95	48,673							
	BG	25,774		S	21,491	-	-	21,491	5,373	
WR	MG	7,345		NS	26,730	9,422	114	36,266	18,133	56,626
	NG	1	33,120							
IR	All Gauges									369,498

Annexure - 9

TRAFFIC UNIT CALCULATIONS : 1991-92

Rev.	Earning NTKM (M) Gauge-wise		Total		PKM (M) BG	MG	NG	Total	TU	Grand Total TU
	BG	41,936		S	20,445	-	-	20,445	5,111	
CR	MG	-		NS	47,258	-	660	47,918	23,959	65,925
	NG	30	41,966							
	BG	25,234		S	14,912	-	-	14,912	3,728	
ER	MG	-		NS	19,261	-	23	19,284	9,642	38,604
	NG	-	25,234							
	BG	38,064		S	38	-	-	38	20	
NR	MG	2,814		NS	42,922	6,517	130	49,569	24,785	65,687
	NG	4	40,882							
	BG	3,082		S	-	-	-	-	-	
NE	MG	4,075		NS	8,601	13,739	-	22,340	11,170	18,327
	NG	-	7,157							
	BG	3,349		S	-	-	-	-	-	
NF	MG	3,224		NS	3,539	3,157	5	6,701	3,351	9,924
	NG	-	6,573							
	BG	10,872		S	1,402	2,173	-	3,575	894	
SR	MG	2,329		NS	17,542	5,894	10	23,446	11,723	25,818
	NG	-	13,201							
	BG	23,374		S	-	-	-	-	-	
SC	MG	2,397		NS	21,903	5,767	-	27,670	13,835	39,606
	NG	-	25,771							
	BG	52,911		S	1,804	-	-	1,804	451	
SE	MG	-		NS	15,062	-	396	15,458	7,729	61,192
	NG	101	53,012							
	BG	28,237		S	22,617	-	-	22,617	5,654	
WR	MG	8,203		NS	28,664	10,001	122	38,787	19,394	61,489
	NG	1	36,441							
IR	All Gauges									386,572

Annexure - 10

TRAFFIC UNIT CALCULATIONS : 1992-93

Rev.	Earning NTKM (M)	Gauge-wise	Total	PKM (M)	BG	MG	NG	Total	TU	Grand Total TU
	BG	41,347		S	19,826	-	-	19,826	4,957	
CR	MG	-		NS	46,468	-	664	47,132	23,566	69,896
	NG	36	41,383							
	BG	26,966		S	14,359	-	-	14,359	3,590	
ER	MG	-		NS	19,684	-	25	19,709	9,855	40,411
	NG	-	26,966					-		
	BG	38,919		S	22	-	-	22	5	
NR	MG	2,610		NS	42,030	4,753	122	46,905	23,453	64,990
	NG	3	41,532							
	BG	2,973		S	-	-	-	-	-	
NE	MG	3,955		NS	9,812	12,706	-	22,518	11,259	18,187
	NG	-	6,928							
	BG	3,086		S	-	-	-	-	-	
NF	MG	3,213		NS	3,650	3,106	6	6,762	3,381	9,680
	NG	-	6,299							
	BG	11,266		S	1,338	2,131	-	3,469	867	
SR	MG	2,356		NS	16,658	4,882	8	21,548	10,774	25,263
	NG	-	13,622							
	BG	24,277		S	-	-	-	-	-	
SC	MG	2,048		NS	20,724	5,042	-	25,766	12,883	39,208
	NG	-	26,325							
	BG	54,461		S	1,383	-	-	1,383	346	
SE	MG	-		NS	12,723	-	380	13,103	6,552	61,456
	NG	97	54,58							
	BG	27,345		S	21,390	-	-	21,390	5,348	
WR	MG	7,431		NS	27,689	8,443	78	36,210	18,105	58,230
	NG	1	34,777							
IR	All Gauges									387,333

Annexure - 11

AVERAGE TRAFFIC UNIT CALCULATION 1988-89/92-93

(Million)

Railway	Traffic Units					Total	Average	% to
	88-89	*89-90*	*90-91*	*91-92*	*92-93*	*TU*	*TU*	*IR*
CR	59612	62490	66424	65925	69896	324347	64869	17.61
ER	37408	37688	37393	38604	40411	191504	38301	10.41
NR	59622	62037	63182	65687	64990	315518	63158	17.14
NE	15919	16924	17381	18327	18187	86738	17348	4.71
NF	8515	9042	9036	9924	9680	46197	9239	2.50
SR	22222	23009	25721	25818	25263	122033	24407	6.63
SC	33639	34865	37176	39606	39208	184494	36899	10.01
SE	51238	55067	56623	61192	61456	285576	57115	15.50
WR	53089	55209	56626	61489	58230	284643	56929	15.46
IR	341264	356331	369498	38572	387333	1840990	368265	100

Annexure - 12

AVERAGE CAPITAL-AT-CHARGE

(Rs.Crore)

Railway	*Capital-at-charge*					*Total*	*Av. Cap.at-Charge*
	1988-89	*1989-90*	*1990-91*	*1991-92*	*1992-93*		
CR	1564.96	1768.93	1933.20	2043.52	2272.77	9583.38	1916.68
ER	1103.52	1230.08	1308.99	1494.36	1601.20	6738.15	1347.63
NR	1732.73	2003.61	2246.73	2513.55	2961.02	11457.64	2291.53
NE	484.65	551.75	611.65	681.52	769.02	3098.59	619.72
NF	609.61	694.29	786.97	882.40	990.83	3964.10	792.82
SR	1075.55	1191.01	1320.45	1423.42	1796.23	6806.66	1361.33
SC	1214.27	1351.91	1453.42	1594.24	1899.27	7513.11	1502.62
SE	1837.48	2004.88	2162.20	2369.11	2686.60	11060.27	2212.06
WR	1275.09	1380.86	1500.56	1576.63	1694.32	7427.46	1485.49
IR	10897.86	12177.32	13324.17	14578.75	16671.26	67649.36	13529.87

NR capital excludes investments in PSUs.

Annexure - 13

AVERAGE TOTAL INVESTMENT 1988-89/92-93

(Rs. Crores)

Rly.	1	2	3	4	5	6	7
CR	20002.85	1699.09	1400.24	808.40	574.63	24485.21	4897.04
ER	17127.10	1447.44	1036.67	749.90	488.19	20849.30	4169.86
NR	19152.90	2122.92	1883.74	1275.45	756.44	25191.45	5038.29
NE	6434.80	730.56	612.89	414.09	203.99	8396.33	1679.27
NF	6696.15	628.13	549.29	385.44	235.25	8494.26	1698.85
SR	13347.05	1154.45	990.45	732.17	589.89	16814.01	3362.80
SC	13521.95	1127.47	852.14	660.65	538.58	16700.79	3340.16
SE	21733.70	1647.53	1246.53	994.04	781.90	26403.70	5280.74
WR	17083.85	1472.36	1042.60	611.28	377.07	20587.16	4117.43
IR	135100.25	12029.95	9614.55	6631.42	4545.94	167922.21	33582.44

Note: 1
Col.1 = Total Inv. 88-89 x 5
Col.2 = Incremental Inv. 89-90 x 4
Col.3 = Incremental Inv. 90-91 x 3
Col.4 = Incremental Inv. 91-92 x 2
Col.5 = Incremental Inv. 92-93 x 1
Col.6 = Total of Col. 1 to Col. 5
Col.7 = $\text{Average} = \frac{\text{Total}}{5}$

Note: 2
For Total Investment upto 1988-89 please see Annexure-22
For Investments in other years please see Annexures 26 to 34

Annexure - 14

CAPITAL INVESTMENT AND TRAFFIC UNIT SHARE 1970-71 / 80-81

Rly.	1970-71			1980-81		Incremental		Inv. Share
	Cap.	*TU*	*TU Ratio*	*Cap.*	*TU*	*Amt.*	*Ratio*	
CR	440.96	24667	15.04	834.37	44079	393.41	14.92	E
ER	447.75	20238	12.34	657.26	24810	209.51	7.95	L
NR	453.52	26599	16.22	803.86	41358	350.34	13.28	L
NE	110.23	8564	5.22	237.72	10657	127.49	4.84	E
NF	202.16	4990	3.04	284.44	5464	82.28	3.12	E
SR	324.12	12938	7.89	597.95	16044	273.83	10.39	H
SC	199.89	14228	8.68	577.33	23073	377.44	14.32	H
SE	668.78	26446	16.13	1118.50	30508	449.72	17.06	E
WR	371.35	25322	15.44	743.70	40674	372.35	14.12	E
IR	3218.76	163992	100.00	5855.13	236667	2636.37	100.00	

NOTE : Capital in Crores of Rupees and TU in Million.

Annexure - 15

CAPITAL INVESTMENT AND TRAFFIC UNIT SHARE 1980-81/88-89

Rly.	*1980-81*			*1988-89*		*Incremental*		*Inv. Share*
	Cap.	*TU*	*TU Ratio*	*Cap.*	*TU*	*Amt.*	*Ratio*	
CR	834.37	44079	18.62	1565.93	59612	731.60	14.52	L
ER	657.26	24810	10.48	1230.30	37408	573.04	11.38	E
NR	803.86	41358	17.48	1597.57	59622	793.71	15.76	E
NE	237.72	10657	4.50	484.65	15919	246.93	4.90	E
NF	284.44	5464	2.31	609.61	8515	325.17	6.46	H
SR	597.95	16044	6.78	1075.55	22222	477.60	9.48	H
SC	577.33	23073	9.75	1214.27	33639	636.94	12.65	H
SE	1118.50	30508	12.89	1837.95	51238	719.45	14.29	H
WR	743.70	40674	17.19	1275.09	53089	531.39	10.56	L
IR	5855.13	236667	100.00	10890.92	341264	5035.83	100.00	

NOTE : Capital in Crores of Rupees & TU in Million.
Capital of NR excludes investments in IRFC & CONCOR

Annexure - 16

CAPITAL INVESTMENT AND TRAFFIC UNIT SHARE 1970-71/88-89

Rly.	*1970-71*			*1988-89*		*Incremental*		*Inv. Share*
	Cap.	*TU*	*TU Ratio*	*Cap.*	*TU*	*Amt.*	*Ratio*	
CR	440.96	24667	15.04	1565.93	59612	1124.97	14.66	E
ER	447.75	20238	12.34	1230.30	36408	782.55	10.20	L
NR	453.52	26599	16.22	1597.57	59622	1144.05	14.91	E
NE	110.23	8564	5.22	484.65	15919	374.42	4.88	E
NF	202.16	4990	3.04	609.61	8515	407.45	5.31	H
SR	324.12	12938	7.89	1075.55	22222	751.43	9.79	H
SC	199.89	14228	8.68	1214.27	33639	1014.38	13.22	H
SE	668.78	26446	16.13	1837.95	51238	1169.17	15.24	E
WR	371.35	25322	15.44	1275.09	53089	903.74	11.78	L
IR	3218.76	163992	100.00	10890.92	341264	7672.16	100.00	

NOTE : Capital in Crores of Rupees & TU in Million.
Capital of NR excludes investments in IRFC & CONCOR

Annexure - 17

AVERAGE CAPITAL-AT-CHARGE AND TRAFFIC UNIT SHARE 1988-89/92-93

(Rs.Crores)

Railway	Av. Cap. 1988-89/92-93	Capital 1992-93	Incremental Cap.	Incremental Ratio	Av. TU Ratio 1988-89/92-93	Inv. Share
CR	1916.68	2272.77	356.09	11.34	17.62	L
ER	1347.63	1601.20	253.57	8.07	10.42	L
NR	2291.53	2961.02	669.49	21.31	17.15	H
NE	619.72	769.02	149.30	4.75	4.71	E
NF	792.82	990.83	198.01	6.30	2.51	H
SR	1361.33	1796.23	434.90	13.84	6.63	H
SC	1502.62	1899.27	396.65	12.64	10.01	H
SE	2212.06	2686.60	474.40	15.10	15.50	E
WR	1485.49	1694.32	208.83	6.65	15.46	L
IR	13529.87	16671.26	3141.39	100	100	

Note : For Av. TU Ratio See Annexure-11

Annexure - 18

PRODUCTIVITY OF CAPITAL-AT-CHARGE : 1970-71/1980-81

Rly.	1970-71		1980-81		Incremental		Indices		ACOR 80-81	ICOR	INDCOR	INDICOR
	Cap.	TU	Cap.	TU	Cap.	TU	Cap.	TU				
CR	440.96	24667	834.37	44079	393.41	19412	189.22	178.70	5.28 H	4.93 H	0.94 H	0.88 H
ER	447.75	20238	657.26	24810	209.51	4572	146.79	122.59	3.77 L	2.18 L	0.84 H	0.48 L
NR	453.52	26599	803.86	41358	350.34	14759	177.25	155.49	5.14 H	4.21 H	0.88 H	0.72 H
NE	110.23	8564	237.72	10657	127.49	2093	215.66	124.44	4.48 L	1.64 L	0.58 L	0.21 L
NF	202.16	4990	284.44	5464	82.28	474	140.70	109.48	1.92 L	0.58 L	0.78 E	0.23 L
SR	324.12	12938	597.95	16044	273.83	3106	184.48	124.00	2.68 L	1.13 L	0.67 L	0.28 L
SC	199.89	14228	577.33	23073	377.44	8845	288.82	162.17	3.99 E	2.34 L	0.56 L	0.33 L
SE	668.78	26446	1118.50	30508	449.72	4062	167.24	115.36	2.73 L	0.90 L	0.69 L	0.23 L
WR	371.35	25322	743.70	40674	372.35	15352	200.27	160.63	5.47 H	4.12 H	0.80 E	0.60 H
IR	3218.76	163992	5855.13	236667	2636.37	72675	181.91	144.32	4.04	2.76	0.79	0.54

NOTE : Capital in Crores of Rupees and TU in Million.
Capital of NR excludes investments in IRFC and CONCOR

Annexure - 19

PRODUCTIVITY OF CAPITAL-AT-CHARGE : 1980-81/1988-89

Rly.	1980-81		1988-89		Incremental		Indices		ACOR 88-89	ICOR	INDCOR	INDICOR
	Cap.	TU	Cap.	TU	Cap.	TU	Cap.	TU				
CR	834.37	44079	1565.93	59612	731.60	15533	187.6	135.2	3.80 H	2.12 E	0.72 E	0.40 L
ER	657.26	24810	1230.30	37408	573.04	12598	187.1	150.8	3.04 E	2.20 E	0.81 E	0.58 H
NR	803.86	41358	1597.57	59622	793.71	18264	198.7	144.2	3.73 H	2.30 H	0.73 E	0.45 L
NE	237.72	10657	484.65	15919	246.93	5262	203.8	149.3	3.28 E	2.13 E	0.73 E	0.48 E
NF	284.44	5464	609.61	8515	325.17	3051	214.3	155.8	1.39 L	0.94 L	0.73 E	0.49 E
SR	597.95	16044	1075.55	22222	477.60	6178	179.8	138.5	2.07 L	1.29 L	0.77 E	0.48 E
SC	577.33	23073	1214.27	33639	636.94	10566	210.3	145.7	2.77 L	1.66 L	0.69 L	0.42 L
SE	1118.50	30508	1837.95	51238	719.45	20730	164.3	167.9	2.79 L	2.88 H	1.02 H	1.06 H
WR	743.70	40674	1275.09	53089	531.39	12415	171.4	130.5	4.16 H	2.34 H	0.76 E	0.43 L
IR	5855.13	236667	10890.92	341264	5035.83	104597	186.0	144.2	3.13	2.08	0.78	0.52

Note : Capital in Crores of Rupees & TU in Million
Capital of NR excludes investments in IRFC & CONCOR

Annexure - 20

PRODUCTIVITY OF CAPITAL-AT-CHARGE : 1970-71/1988-89

Rly.	1970-71		1988-89		Incremental		Indices		ACOR 88-89	ICOR	INDCOR	INDICOR
	Cap.	TU	Cap.	TU	Cap.	TU	Cap.	TU				
CR	440.96	24667	1565.93	59612	1124.97	34945	355.1	241.7	3.80 H	3.11 H	0.68 H	0.56 H
ER	447.75	20238	1230.30	37408	782.55	17170	274.7	184.8	3.04 E	2.19 E	0.67 E	0.49 H
NR	453.52	26599	1597.57	59622	1144.05	33023	352.2	224.1	3.73 H	2.89 H	0.64 E	0.49 H
NE	110.23	8564	484.65	15919	374.42	7355	439.6	185.9	3.28 E	1.96 L	0.42 L	0.25 L
NF	202.16	4990	609.61	8515	407.45	3525	301.5	170.6	1.39 L	0.87 L	0.57 E	0.35 L
SR	324.12	12938	1075.55	22222	751.43	9284	331.8	171.7	2.07 L	1.24 L	0.52 L	0.31 L
SC	199.89	14228	1214.27	33639	1014.38	19411	607.4	236.4	2.77 L	1.91 L	0.39 L	0.27 L
SE	668.78	26446	1837.95	51238	1169.17	24792	274.8	193.7	2.79 L	2.12 E	0.71 H	0.54 H
WR	371.35	25322	1275.09	53089	903.74	27767	343.3	209.7	4.16 H	3.07 H	0.61 E	0.45 E
IR	3218.76	163992	10890.92	341264	7672.16	177272	338.3	208.1	3.13	2.31	0.62	0.45

NOTE : Capital in Crores of Rupees & TU in Million.
Capital of NR excludes investments in IRFC & CONCOR

Annexure - 21

PRODUCTIVITY OF CAPITAL-AT-CHARGE : 1988-89/1992-93

Rly.	*Av. 88-89/92-93*		*1992-93*		*Incremental*		*Indices*		*ACOR 92-93*	*ICOR*	*INDCOR*	*INDICOR*
	Cap.	*TU*	*Cap.*	*TU*	*Cap.*	*TU*	*Cap.*	*TU*				
CR	1916.68	64869	2272.77	69896	356.09	5027	118.58	107.75	3.08 H	1.41 H	0.909 E	0.417 H
ER	1347.63	38301	1601.20	40411	253.57	2110	118.16	105.51	2.52 E	0.83 H	0.893 E	0.292 E
NR	2370.76	63158	2478.76	64990	108.00	1832	104.56	102.90	2.62 E	1.70 H	0.984 H	0.639 H
NE	619.72	17348	769.02	18187	149.30	839	124.09	104.84	2.36 E	0.56 L	0.845 E	0.200 L
NF	792.82	9239	990.83	9680	198.01	441	124.98	104.77	0.98 L	0.22 L	0.838 E	0.168 L
SR	1361.33	24407	1796.23	25263	434.90	856	131.95	103.51	1.41 L	0.20 L	0.784 L	0.112 L
SC	1502.62	36899	1899.27	39208	396.65	2309	126.40	106.26	2.06 L	0.58 L	0.841 E	0.236 L
SE	2212.06	57115	2686.60	61456	474.54	4341	121.45	107.60	2.29 E	0.91 H	0.886 E	0.353 H
WR	1485.49	56929	1694.32	58230	208.83	1301	114.06	102.29	3.44 H	0.62 L	0.897 E	0.161 L
IR	13609.11	368265	16189.00	387321	2579.89	19056	118.96	105.17	2.39	0.74	0.884	0.273

Note:- Amount is Rs. Crores and TU in Millions

Capital of NR excludes investments in PSUs

Annexure - 22

TOTAL INVESTMENTS AND TRAFFIC UNIT SHARE : 1980-81/1988-89

Rly.	1980-81			1980-81/1988-89		
	Block Act.	*TU*	*TU Ratio*	*Incr. Inv.*	*Ratio*	*Inv. Share*
CR	1010.26	44079	18.62	2990.31	15.08	L
ER	814.14	24810	10.48	2611.28	13.17	H
NR	1000.71	41358	17.48	2829.89	14.27	L
NE	360.44	10657	4.50	926.52	4.67	E
NF	352.34	5464	2.31	986.89	4.98	H
SR	728.10	16044	6.78	1941.31	9.97	H
SC	690.57	23073	9.75	2013.82	10.16	E
SE	1256.13	30508	12.89	3090.61	15.58	H
WR	977.36	40674	17.26	2439.41	12.30	L
IR	7190.03	235667	100	19830.02		

Note - Incr.Inv = Incremental (Capital + DRF + DF + OLWR + ACSPF) between 1980-81 and 88-89.

Annexure - 23

AVERAGE TOTAL INVESTMENT AND TRAFFIC UNIT SHARE 1988-89/92/93

Railway	*Av. Total Inv. 1988-89/92-93*	*Total Inv. 1992-93*	*Incremental Inv.*	*Incremental Ratio*	*Av. TU Ratio 1988-89/92-93*	*Inv. Share*
CR	4897.04	5870.92	973.88	12.12	17.62	L
ER	4169.86	4995.98	826.12	11.13	10.42	E
NR	5038.29	6383.39	1345.10	18.12	17.15	E
NE	1679.27	2084.93	405.66	5.46	4.71	H
NF	1698.85	2021.73	322.88	4.35	2.50	H
SR	3362.80	4244.14	881.34	11.87	6.63	H
SC	3340.16	4139.21	799.05	10.76	10.01	E
SE	5280.74	6453.05	1172.31	15.79	15.50	E
WR	4117.43	4815.10	697.67	9.40	15.46	L
IR	33582.44	41006.45	7424.01	100	100	

Note: For Av. TU Ratio see Annexure-11.
For Av. Total Investment see Annexure-13

Annexure - 24

PRODUCTIVITY OF TOTAL INVESTMENTS : 1980-81/1988-89

Rly.	1980-81		1988-89		Incremental		Indices		ACOR 88-89	ICOR	INDCOR	INDICOR
	Block Act.	TU	Total Inv.	TU	Inv.	TU	Inv.	TU				
CR	1010.26	44079	4000.57	59612	2990.31	15533	400.0	135.2	1.49 H	0.52 E	0.34 E	0.117 L
ER	814.14	24810	3425.42	37408	2611.28	12598	420.8	150.8	1.09 L	0.48 E	0.36 E	0.158 E
NR	1000.71	41358	3830.58	59622	2829.89	18264	382.8	144.2	1.56 H	0.65 H	0.38 E	0.156 E
NE	360.44	10657	1286.96	15919	926.52	5262	357.1	149.3	1.23 E	0.57 E	0.42 H	0.192 H
NF	352.34	5464	1339.23	8515	986.89	3051	380.1	155.8	0.64 L	0.31 L	0.41 E	0.199 H
SR	728.10	16044	2669.41	22222	1941.31	6178	366.6	138.5	0.83 L	0.32 L	0.38 E	0.144 E
SC	690.57	23073	2704.39	33639	2013.82	10566	391.6	145.7	1.24 E	0.52 E	0.37 E	0.157 E
SE	1256.13	30508	4346.74	51238	3090.61	20730	346.0	167.9	1.18 E	0.67 H	0.49 H	0.276 H
WR	977.36	40674	3416.77	53089	2439.41	12415	349.6	130.5	1.55 H	0.51 E	0.37 E	0.122 L
IR	7190.03	236667	27020.05	341264	19830.02	104597	375.8	144.2	1.26	0.53	0.38	0.161

Note : Investment in Crores of Rupees & TU in Million

Investment of NR excludes investments in IRFC & CONCOR

Total Investment in 1988-89 = Block Account in 1980-81 plus Total Additional Investment between 1980-81 and 1988-89

Annexure - 25

PRODUCTIVITY OF AVERAGE TOTAL INVESTMENTS : 1988-89/1992-93

Rly.	*Average Inv.*	*Total TU*	*1992-93*		*Incremental*		*Indices*		*ACOR 92-93*	*ICOR*	*INDCOR*	*INDICOR*
			Inv.	*TU*	*Inv.*	*TU*	*Inv.*	*TU*				
CR	4897.04	64869	5870.92	69896	973.88	5027	119.89	107.75	1.191 H	0.516 H	0.899 E	0.389 H
ER	4169.86	38301	4995.98	40411	826.12	2110	119.81	105.51	0.809 L	0.255 E	0.881 E	0.277 H
NR	5038.29	63158	6383.39	64990	1345.10	1832	126.70	102.90	1.018 E	0.136 L	0.812 E	0.108 L
NE	1679.27	17348	2084.93	18187	405.66	839	124.16	104.84	0.872 E	0.207 L	0.844 E	0.200 L
NF	1698.85	9239	2021.73	9680	322.88	441	119.01	104.77	0.479 L	0.137 L	0.880 E	0.252 E
SR	3362.80	24407	4244.14	25263	881.34	856	121.21	103.51	0.595 L	0.097 L	0.820 E	0.134 L
SC	3340.16	36899	4139.21	39208	799.05	2309	123.92	106.26	0.947 E	0.289 H	0.857 E	0.262 H
SE	5280.74	57115	6453.05	61456	1172.31	4341	122.20	107.60	0.952 E	0.370 H	0.881 E	0.342 H
WR	4117.43	56929	4815.10	58230	697.67	1301	116.94	102.29	1.209 H	0.186 L	0.875 E	0.134 L
IR	33584.44	368265	41008.45	387321	7424.01	19056	122.11	105.17	0.944	0.257	0.861	0.234

Note:- Amount in Rs. Crores and TU in Millions

Investments on NR exclude Investments by NR in PSUs.

Annexure - 26

INVESTMENTS ON CENTRAL RAILWAY

[Rs.Thousand]

YEAR	*CAPITAL*	*DRF*	*DF*	*ACSPF*	*OLWR*	*TOTAL*
1980-81	741186	377939	37815	15384	9643	1181967
1981-82	809274	854111	32667	16355	10094	1722501
1982-83	633799	959888	37786	27385	9441	1668299
1983-84	565583	1662275	39419	27577	8241	2303095
1984-85	443175	1444765	66585	35882	13431	2003838
1985-86	697556	1712100	85470	39782	18063	2552971
1986-87	1529752	1786781	187323	55914	28976	3588746
1987-88	1126014	1376187	201650	64544	37677	2806072
1988-89	1527235	2272357	151130	70684	31601	4053007
1989-90	1975011	1964850	170096	104987	32786	4247730
1990-91	1587205	2739844	222675	87365	30365	4667454
1991-92	1088905	2659660	1874909	73985	31986	4042027
1992-93	2292530	3136663	211775	69680	35616	5746264
TOTAL	15017225	22947420	3319300	689524	297920	40583971

Annexure - 27

INVESTMENTS ON EASTERN RAILWAY

[Rs.Thousand]

YEAR	CAPITAL	DRF	DF	ACSPF	OLWR	TOTAL
1980-81	549679	510257	46600	11835	9861	1128232
1981-82	515900	877568	47457	9843	7423	1458191
1982-83	189956	914104	48829	23375	11868	1188132
1983-84	122061	1333189	57936	25084	8689	1546959
1984-85	195896	1429582	53588	27899	14729	1721694
1985-86	1315094	1360068	72261	33053	14476	2794952
1986-87	1594765	1833535	139679	37694	25317	3630990
1987-88	614851	1742333	165987	69665	35041	2627877
1988-89	1104041	1989133	125225	68736	49786	3336921
1989-90	1224809	2138147	147367	60319	47955	3618597
1990-91	1026337	2099707	215769	63908	49818	3455539
1991-92	1088049	2396021	147145	69267	49024	3749506
1992-93	1071438	3519981	146617	112732	31162	4881930
Total	10612876	22143625	1414460	613410	355149	35139520

Annexure - 28

INVESTMENTS ON NORTHERN RAILWAY

[Rs.Thousand]

YEAR	CAPITAL	DRF	DF	ACSPF	OLWR	TOTAL
1980-81	759733	274463	39936	17612	16352	1108096
1981-82	581001	452225	31051	19890	10277	1094444
1982-83	673979	616395	49040	31104	10285	1380803
1983-84	331949	713148	36268	32966	12434	1126765
1984-85	1229291	1326333	62298	41833	18439	2678194
1985-86	729718	1502127	68544	41954	17965	2360308
1986-87	1965801	1770741	176577	55938	28100	3997157
1987-88	2041144	1711830	201189	64310	40738	4059211
1988-89	2204644	2130591	188232	80871	82962	4687300
1989-90	2888469	1987846	264008	72499	94489	5307311
1990-91	2383930	3414994	293333	94027	92838	6279122
1991-92	2960863	3089614	193016	52293	81482	6377268
1992-93	3834712	3249138	339038	68607	72906	7564401
Total	22585234	22239445	1942530	673904	579267	48020380

Note : Includes investment in PSUs

	Rs. (Crores)
88-89	64.84
89-90	85.00
90-91	80.33
91-92	115.00
92-93	51.00

Annexure - 29

INVESTMENTS ON NORTH EASTERN RAILWAY

[Rs.Thousand]

YEAR	CAPITAL	DRF	DF	ACSPF	OLWR	TOTAL
1980-81	432556	117863	30041	4154	7557	592171
1981-82	339325	217615	32011	8106	7449	604506
1982-83	139271	203087	25596	9897	9764	387615
1983-84	130696	232940	42005	7756	11713	425110
1984-85	312433	359110	40038	14831	12950	739362
1985-86	200058	246372	37230	10297	11110	505067
1986-87	507540	462134	86091	19519	19723	1095007
1987-88	356839	575360	91910	29466	21517	1075092
1988-89	492086	1112957	76901	34445	29919	1746308
1989-90	661658	1006954	80186	46142	31450	1826390
1990-91	598958	1328859	57908	35350	21902	2042977
1991-92	698764	1305095	23430	31504	11672	2070465
1992-93	874984	1095043	31153	27742	10934	2039856
Total	5745168	8263389	654500	654500	207660	15149926

Annexure - 30

INVESTMENTS ON NORTHEAST FRONTIER RAILWAY

[Rs.Thousand]

YEAR	*CAPITAL*	*DRF*	*DF*	*ACSPF*	*OLWR*	*TOTAL*
1980-81	297847	166783	7710	1058	4943	478341
1981-82	315558	188828	8287	1218	6043	519934
1982-83	266257	183264	10214	1804	5009	466548
1983-84	209731	176066	16376	1369	4817	408359
1984-85	324089	259575	10980	2947	4854	602445
1985-86	426383	358853	19004	3994	6940	815174
1986-87	417237	668234	36578	10257	15342	1147648
1987-88	741495	531960	45300	21605	23727	1364087
1988-89	799238	720152	30906	15444	22286	1588026
1989-90	846827	638358	45716	15264	24154	1570319
1990-91	926765	804855	54744	17634	26959	1830957
1991-92	951113	879592	57958	13379	25137	1927179
1992-93	1084252	1169256	67197	5536	26280	2352521
Total	7606792	6745776	410970	111509	196491	15071538

Annexure - 31

INVESTMENTS ON SOUTHERN RAILWAY

[Rs.Thousand]

YEAR	CAPITAL	DRF	DF	ACSPF	OLWR	TOTAL
1980-81	457197	334095	33984	13740	10662	849678
1981-82	357365	417423	35580	13450	14134	837952
1982-83	435988	654048	48727	26613	12029	1177405
1983-84	473214	631530	40165	38614	13940	1197463
1984-85	603376	581633	53646	28725	10882	1278262
1985-86	545133	782170	51081	31027	1280	1410691
1986-87	727940	927015	80635	54458	32928	1822976
1987-88	602747	1284782	122775	56308	38197	2104809
1988-89	886735	1495657	185975	59740	48018	2676125
1989-90	1092317	1542226	146500	57295	47795	2886133
1990-91	1254170	1817669	122192	74859	32624	3301514
1991-92	1044683	2406079	111632	67300	31131	3660825
1992-93	3616809	2105874	96409	57581	22200	5898873
Total	12097674	14980201	1129301	579710	315820	29102706

Annexure - 32

INVESTMENTS ON SOUTH CENTRAL RAILWAY

[Rs.Thousand]

YEAR	*CAPITAL*	*DRF*	*DF*	*ACSPF*	*OLWR*	*TOTAL*
1980-81	680061	336176	29206	12447	10874	1068764
1981-82	822587	477234	25950	15289	10900	1351960
1982-83	812870	662641	29998	32261	10612	1548382
1983-84	755718	506720	26643	22985	10505	1322571
1984-85	1386042	578825	24716	21641	12792	2024016
1985-86	898481	883512	28584	10777	9551	1830905
1986-87	1570544	916130	36400	37566	22312	2582952
1987-88	946012	1122846	58680	33653	32264	2193455
1988-89	1083203	1347097	120889	52084	36448	2639721
1989-90	1370666	1254530	79683	68483	45319	2818681
1990-91	1047239	1609262	66968	80050	36937	2840456
1991-92	1388620	1737680	58100	89559	29275	3303234
1992-93	3073481	2146929	60368	79128	25889	5385795
Total	15835524	13579582	646185	555923	293678	30910892

Annexure - 33

INVESTMENTS ON SOUTH EASTERN RAILWAY

[Rs.Thousand]

YEAR	CAPITAL	DRF	DF	ACSPF	OLWR	TOTAL
1980-81	897369	355551	23664	9493	10980	1297057
1981-82	573941	1034692	20172	14070	11095	1653970
1982-83	526141	1518782	29638	16375	11684	2102620
1983-84	779388	1590571	31349	22154	10824	2434286
1984-85	859482	804791	32676	22197	16311	1735457
1985-86	400003	1515276	30827	33254	13211	1992571
1986-87	1488956	1706465	54372	24324	26806	3300923
1987-88	1323865	1460912	61978	24034	32796	2903585
1988-89	1874645	1427599	73707	26616	28168	3430735
1989-90	1785649	2180360	77701	44961	30158	4118829
1990-91	1479516	2484974	102228	56182	32207	4155107
1991-92	2095608	2697793	89285	55959	31365	4970010
1992-93	3174916	4424588	102615	92038	24853	7819010
Total	17259479	23202354	730212	441657	280458	41914160

Annexure - 34

INVESTMENTS ON WESTERN RAILWAY

[Rs.Thousand]

YEAR	*CAPITAL*	*DRF*	*DF*	*ACSPF*	*OLWR*	*TOTAL*
1980-81	678169	300504	48029	20481	16171	1063354
1981-82	674791	483793	39114	15310	11975	1224983
1982-83	510825	794069	47261	17869	13121	1383145
1983-84	642827	937230	36269	23375	14097	1653798
1984-85	442934	1092610	33254	17599	9728	1596125
1985-86	786872	1350658	28030	22906	23049	2211515
1986-87	738572	1494685	36082	43458	34770	2347567
1987-88	911118	61800034	85528	63758	48496	2908934
1988-89	983599	2038933	107281	69535	39358	3238706
1989-90	980480	2457737	141259	48885	52544	3680905
1990-91	1183615	2067814	86440	86583	50879	3475331
1991-92	760705	2023691	104710	127846	39432	3056384
1992-93	1265084	2187699	110041	151102	56760	3770686
Total	10559591	19029457	903298	708707	410380	31611433

Annexure - 35

OPERATING EXPENSES PER TRAFFIC UNIT : 1980-81/92-93

Rly.		*1980-81*			*1992-93*		*Index of*
	Op.Exp.(Cr)	*TU (M)*	*Exp.per TU*	*Op.Exp(Cr)*	*TU(M)*	*Exp.per TU*	*Increase*
CR	379.63	44079	0.086	1514.00	69896	0.217	252.33
ER	348.89	24810	0.141	1329.01	40411	0.329	233.33
NR	422.06	41358	0.102	1656.91	64990	0.255	250.00
NE	133.10	10657	0.125	546.56	18187	0.301	240.08
NF	127.40	5464	0.233	427.84	9680	0.442	189.70
SR	245.51	16044	0.151	817.33	25263	0.324	214.57
SC	239.57	23073	0.104	903.42	39208	0.230	221.15
SE	325.53	30508	0.107	1448.79	61456	0.236	220.56
WR	353.95	40674	0.087	1275.92	58230	0.219	251.72
IR	2575.64	236667	0.109	991978	387321	0.256	234.86

Note - Operating Expenses include only such Heads of Demand which are affected by DRF exspenditure viz. Demands 4 to 12.

For Heads of Demands for Grants please see Annexure-2.

Annexure - 36

DENSITY OF TRAFFIC 1988-89/1992-93

	1980 - 81			1988-89 / 92-93		
Rly.	*EQTKM*	*TU(M)*	*DENSITY*	*EQTKM*	*Av. TU (M)*	*DENSITY*
CR	15905.46	44079	2.77	19194.75	64869	3.37
ER	13281.20	24810	1.87	15761.57	38301	2.43
NR	18120.92	41358	2.28	18683.93	63158	3.38
NE	6739.92	10657	1.58	6849.17	17348	2.53
NF	5826.01	5464	0.94	6452.23	9239	1.43
SR	9820.38	16044	1.63	11494.94	24407	2.12
SC	12062.71	23073	1.91	14334.86	36899	2.57
SE	19850.67	30508	1.54	21558.75	57115	2.65
WR	16671.50	40674	2.44	17069.57	56929	3.34
IR	117978.83	236667	2.00	131399.77	368265	2.80

Note - EQTKM = ETKMs of Running Track Km + Transportation Siding + Marshalling Yard + Coaching Yard.

Annexure - 37

SANCTIONED AND PROJECTED RESOURCE ALLOCATION 1995-96 (Gross)

(Rs.Lakhs)

RLY.	*ACTUAL ALLOCATION 1995-96*							*PROJECTED ALLOTMENT*	
	Cap.	*DRF*	*DF*	*Cap.Fund*	*OLWR*	*Total*	*%*	*Av. TU Ratio 88-89/92-93*	*Amount*
CR	2942	29556	4672	72705	345	110270	13.21	17.61	146948
ER	2118	22576	4555	71266	329	100844	12.08	10.41	86867
NR	5226	24912	4052	92394	727	127611	15.29	17.14	143026
NE	120	7571	1673	29863	328	39555	4.74	4.71	39303
NF	24621	17295	1382	-	402	43700	5.24	2.56	21362
SR	1215	18125	2395	58724	511	80975	9.70	6.62	55241
SC	377	27396	6198	64493	389	98853	11.85	10.01	83529
SE	7249	38835	3779	74491	543	124897	14.97	15.49	129259
WR	1462	25149	3904	76642	598	107755	12.92	15.45	128925
IR						834460			834460

Note:- 1. NR investment excludes investment in PSUs Rs. 10.00 crores.

BIBLIOGRAPHY & SOURCES OF DATA

Bibliography

1. Railway Reforms Committee Report Part XXII on Traffic Costing and Railway Statistics.
2. Report of the Committee on Capital Output Ratio for Indian Railways 1988.
3. Report of the Productivity Linked Bonus Reveiw Committee Sept., 1985.
4. Verma, K.B., 'Marginal Productivity of Railway Investments Part 1', Rail Transport, June 1991.
5. Verma, K.B., 'Marginal Productivity of Railway Investments Part 2', Rail Transport, September 1991
6. Chitale, V.P., 'Capital Output Ratios in the Indian Economy, 1986. Economic and Scientific Research Foundation. Published by Radiant Publishers, New Delhi.

Sources of Data

1. For Traffic Unit Calculations.
   Statement Nos. 12 and 13 of Indian Railways. Annual Statistical Statement of different years.
2. For Capital-at-Charge
   Explanatory Memorandum to Railway Budget.
3. For Block Account.
   Statement 3 of Indian Railways Annual Statistical Statements.
4. For Other Investments.
   Accounts Directorate of Ministry of Railways.

Index